Carta's Illustrated Encyclopedia of the Holy Temple in Jerusalem

Pilgrims approach their long-awaited destination: the Temple Mount.

Carta's Illustrated Encyclopedia of the Holy Temple in Jerusalem

Israel Ariel
Chaim Richman

The Temple Institute
Carta, Jerusalem

Israel Ariel and Chaim Richman
CARTA'S ILLUSTRATED ENCYCLOPEDIA OF THE HOLY TEMPLE IN JERUSALEM

Co-published by The Temple Institute and Carta, Jerusalem

All drawings, photographs and designs prepared by The Temple Institute

Translated and adapted from the Hebrew: Yehoshua Wertheimer

Content adviser: Rabbi Menahem Makover
Editor: Barbara Ball
Art director: Eli Kellerman
Design: Uzi Dor

Drawings: Zalman Smekhov, George Berdichevsky, Dmitry Baranovsky, Grigory Vechlis, and Michael Putilov
Artisans: Gadi Nataf and Chaim Odem (gold and silver vessels); Landau Castings Ltd. (copper and bronze vessels); S. Mishali "Y'dei Uman" (copper vessels); Harrari Family (musical instruments); Baruch Blumin (gold artwork)
Photographs: Ya'acov Harlap

Plates: Mixam, Tel Aviv
Printers: Meiri, Holon
Bookbinders: Weiss, Beth Shemesh

Carta, Jerusalem
18 Ha'uman Street, POB 2500, Jerusalem 91024, Israel
Phone: 972-2-678-3355 Fax: 972-2-678-2373
E-mail: carta@carta.co.il
Website: holyland-jerusalem.com

ISBN: 965-220-530-3

Printed in Israel

Introduction
A Heavenly Vision of the Temple

Better is the sight of the eyes than the wandering of the desire. (Eccl. 6:9)

Visual representation is an important element in the learning process. This is all the more true when treating topics such as the Holy Temple. Even Moses, the greatest of all prophets, set about building the desert Tabernacle and its furnishings only after he was first granted a heavenly vision of this structure in fine detail—as Scripture states, "They shall make me a Sanctuary, and I will dwell among them. You shall make the Tabernacle and all of its furnishings *according to the plan that I show you*" (Ex. 25:8–9).

In days gone by, when the people of Israel would journey to the Holy City to celebrate the Pilgrim Festivals, they would stand awestruck at the sight of the Temple. The Talmud describes how priests would go out of their way to display the Temple's beauty to the many visitors. For example, they would open the Holy of Holies and allow the celebrants to see the cherubim atop the Holy Ark embracing like man and wife. Their embrace indicated Divine predilection, and the priests would therefore exclaim before the people, "See how greatly you are cherished before God!" (*Yoma* 54a).

This, indeed, was one of the objectives of the pilgrimages—to make an indelible impression of the Temple on all who saw it. Visitors, however, would be moved not only by the outer, physical beauty of this imposing edifice; they would be awed by its inner, spiritual content—the all-pervasive Divine Presence.

This profound idea is supported by the words of Maimonides when he tells us that "just as the people of Israel would come to the Temple to appear before God, so they would come to see His splendorous sanctity and the house of His Divine Presence" (*Hilkhot Hagigah* 2:1).

Though laid waste many hundreds of years ago, the Temple has survived in the mind of man. Jews of all generations have persisted in exploring every aspect of its magnificent and complex structure and intricate sacred service. Many have pondered and probed as best they could the mysteries of the Holy Temple, yet they lacked the instruments needed to give concrete form to their studies.

A huge number of thoroughly researched paintings and scaled-to-size gold and silver reproductions of Temple vessels, instruments and vestments are on display at the Temple Institute in Jerusalem, and may be viewed by the public. These amazing works of art have been fashioned by accomplished, contemporary craftsmen. They patiently await the day when priests will take them and ascend the Temple Mount to perform the sacred service in the Holy Temple of God, as in days of old.

The Temple Institute and Carta are proud to present the reader with a panorama of illustrations and photographs, and so provide a detailed visual representation of the Holy Temple. The outstanding and often moving artwork presented here is the fruit of years of effort and patience by scholars and artists under the guidance of Rabbi Israel Ariel.

Much of the material in this book appears here for the very first time. Presented in an organized, systematic, and comprehensive form, it allows all—father and son, teacher and student, scholar and layman—to delve deeply into the subject of the Temple and its vessels. Now, all can partake in a vision of the Temple and its vessels with their own eyes—not unlike Moses himself.

May the chapters of this book be like the virtual gates of the Temple, allowing the reader to enter into the holy Sanctuary and stand before God.

Table of Contents

The Temple: Where History Begins

The sages inform us that the concept of the Holy Temple was an important factor in the Divine act of creation. In fact, the Temple was one of the reasons that the universe was brought into existence. The Almighty "contemplated seven things before creating the universe: Torah, Repentance, the Garden of Eden, Gehenna, the Throne of Glory, the Holy Temple, and the Messiah's identity" (*Pesachim* 54a).

In other words, the Temple represents an essential stage in the spiritual development and moral rectification of all creation. This holy complex and its Divine service have the power to hasten the advent of the Messiah and bring about the final redemption.

There is an ancient tradition which says that the first sacrifice offered on Mount Moriah in Jerusalem was brought by Adam on the day after he was created. Later, Cain and Abel presented offerings to God upon the altar which Adam had built. They were followed by Noah, who in turn was followed by the patriarch Abraham. The offering required of Abraham, however, was different from all others....

The sages direct our attention to the fact that on two separate occasions, Abraham is commanded by God to set out on a journey. In Genesis 12:1, God enjoins the patriarch to leave his birthplace and father's house in the Mesopotamian city of Haran in order to go to the land that God will show him—Canaan, the Land of Israel.

Years later, Abraham is called upon again (ibid. 22: 2). This time he is told to take his beloved son Isaac to Mount Moriah and present him there as a burnt-offering. When a heavenly angel appears to Abraham and prevents him from carrying out the Divine command, he feels compelled to find a substitute. Looking up, he notices a ram caught in some thickets, and sacrifices it "in his son's stead." This episode serves as an archetype for all Temple sacrifice thenceforth. Such service must contain an element of genuine self-sacrifice before God. It was then that Abraham declared the establishment of a Sanctuary on that spot, Mount Moriah.

The sages of the *Midrash* pose a question: which of Abraham's two Divine callings was of greater significance—his trek to the Land of Israel, or his journey to Mount Moriah? They conclude that the second was the more important of the two. Abraham's journey to Mount Moriah, because it paved the way for the establishment of the Holy Temple, was more momentous than his initial emigration to the Land of Israel. "The Holy Temple," say the sages, "is the beautification of the world." When Israel dwells in its land with the Holy Temple functioning in its proper place, beauty and excellence are bestowed upon all humanity.

Hundreds of years later, God frees the Children of Israel from Egyptian bondage. In the desert, at the foot of Mount Sinai, they construct a Sanctuary—the Tabernacle. The day of the Tabernacle's dedication is a zenith in world history. According to the *Midrash*, this date was adorned with ten "crowns." It was the first day of creation; it was the first day that the leaders of the tribes of Israel began to bring their offerings to the Tabernacle; it was the first day that Aaron and his sons began to serve as priests; it was the first day of the Divine service for the Israelites; it was the first day that fire descended from heaven to consume the sacrifices on the altar; it was the first day that Israelites were required to eat their offerings within the boundaries of the Tabernacle's enclosures; it was the first day that the Divine Presence rested on Israel; it was the first day that the Israelites were blessed with the Priestly Blessing; it was the first day that private altars were forbidden; and it was the first day that the New Moon Festival was celebrated.

Through the wilderness and into the Land of Israel, the Sanctuary wandered from place to place with no fixed home for 440 years. Finally, the time arrived for transferring the Sanctuary to its permanent location in Jerusalem. David brought the ark up to the City of David, dug the Temple's foundations, and built an altar on Mount Moriah. Solomon continued his father's work, engaging multitudes in quarrying stone and transporting materials for the building project. Finally, the work was completed. At the dedication ceremony, King Solomon praised the Lord for His abundant kindness and announced that the Holy Temple in Jerusalem was to be at once a place of worship for the Nation of Israel and a house of prayer for all people on Earth.

As we shall see in the illustrations that follow, the First and Second Temple eras were the most glorious in Israel's history. Yet, as noted, the true purpose of the Sanctuary is to be a light and inspiration for all of humanity. May it be God's will that the Temple be speedily restored to its former state of Glory as the soul and conscience of the entire world and the focal point for the prayers of all humanity.

Adam's Offering on Mount Moriah

The Torah teaches that "God formed Adam out of the dust of the ground," and the sages explain that this dust was taken from the very ground upon which the Temple's altar would eventually stand. On the day following his creation—Sabbath—Adam himself built an altar on this spot and offered up a sacrifice. Here, Adam and Eve thank God for bringing them into existence and praise Him for the entire creation. According to tradition, Adam was moved to compose a song at this time which would later be incorporated into the Book of Psalms: "A Song for the Sabbath Day" (Ps. 92).

Cain and Abel On the first anniversary of the world's creation, Cain and Abel presented offerings to God upon the altar which Adam had built. Here, Abel lifts his hands in gratitude at the sight of his sacrifice's acceptance. Cain, however, lowers his face in dejection, for God has paid no heed to his offering.

Noah Offers Sacrifices in the Flood's Aftermath

In Genesis 8:18–20, the Torah describes how Noah, upon leaving the ark, built an altar and offered sacrifices to God. Jewish tradition informs us that Noah's altar was built on Mount Moriah, in the same place that Adam's had previously stood. In this illustration, Noah, surrounded by family members, is about to offer a sacrifice; his sons prepare additional offerings.

The Binding of Isaac on Mount Moriah

Abraham, the father of the Jewish nation, brought an offering to this same altar on Mount Moriah, but the sacrifice required of him was different from all others—he was asked to submit his beloved son as a burnt offering. Abraham thus revealed to the entire world the extent to which one is required to go in dedicating himself to God's honor. Here, father and son behold a vision of the future Sanctuary.

Isaac's Prayer on Mount Moriah

According to the Talmud, Isaac went out to pray on Mount Moriah just as a convoy of camels arrived with his soon-to-be wife, Rebekah (*Berakhot* 26b; *Pesachim* 88a). Here, Isaac lifts his hands in prayer before the Holy Temple's future location. A band of camels bringing Abraham's servant, Eliezer, and Rebekah, is discernible in the background.

Jacob's Dream on Mount Moriah

Many authorities explain that the place where Jacob had his famous dream of a ladder rising to heaven with angels ascending and descending was none other than the future location of the Holy of Holies in Jerusalem. Perceiving this, the patriarch called the place "God's temple" and "the gate to heaven" (Gen. 28:17).

Indeed, according to the *Midrash*, Jacob's dream is itself an allegorical allusion to the Temple service. The angels represent High Priests bringing offerings up the altar's ramp; the fragrance of these offerings "rose up to heaven."

Degrees of Holiness in the Wilderness

The Israelite encampment possessed three principal levels of sanctity. Most holy was the Camp of the Divine Presence, which included the Tabernacle and its enclosure (dark orange); second, the Camp of the Levites (medium orange); and third, the Camp of Israel (light orange).

The Tabernacle and the Tent of Moses

In its detailed description of the Levite camp, the Bible informs us that the tent of Moses was situated opposite the Tabernacle entrance on the eastern side (Num. 3:38). This tent was the meeting place for the seventy elders who comprised the members of Moses' rabbinical court. "All who sought the Lord" would go there (Ex. 33:7).

Here, the Tabernacle is seen from the east, with Moses' tent to the left.

The Tabernacle at the Foot of Mount Sinai

The twelve tribes of Israel surround the mountain, with the Divine "cloud of glory" at its top. This scenario persisted for almost ten months, at which point the Divine cloud left the mountain's summit in order to rest upon the Tabernacle below.

The arrangement of the camp of Israel—namely, the dwelling of the Divine Presence in the center, surrounded by the Camp of the Levites, and encompassed by the Israelite tribes—was permanently established from that time on. Hence, even once in Jerusalem, the order was symbolically maintained, with the Holy Temple in the center, surrounded by the Temple Mount (equivalent to the Levite camp), and encompassed by "the Israelite camp"—the City of Jerusalem.

The Sinai Revelation as a Prototype for the Divine Service in the Holy Temple

As an introduction to the great event of the Giving of the Law at Mount Sinai, Moses built an altar at the foot of the mountain and directed the priests to offer sacrifices thereupon, as it is written, "and he built an altar at the foot of the mountain" (Ex. 24:4). With this action, Moses inaugurated what was later to become the daily service in the Tabernacle—and, ultimately, in the Holy Temple in Jerusalem. Twelve monuments were also erected at the foot of Mount Sinai, for the twelve tribes of Israel.

The Tabernacle at Shilo

Shilo was home to the Tabernacle for 369 years. The Mishnah informs us that at that time the Tabernacle "possessed no roof, but was comprised of a stone structure below and a tent covering above" (*Zevachim* 14:6).

Here, in the center of the courtyard, a son of Eli the Priest is seen holding a three-

pronged fork. "All that the fork brought up the priest took for himself" (1 Sam. 2:14).
To the right (in blue) a woman raises her hands in prayer in a manner reminiscent of Hannah, mother of Samuel the Prophet.

Samuel and David Identify the Temple Site

The night that David fled King Saul and took shelter in the house of Samuel the Prophet is described by the sages as "a night that abounded in Torah study." The *Midrash* relates: "On the night that David escaped from Saul, he learned things from Samuel that even experienced Torah scholars do not learn in a hundred years" (*Yalkut Shimoni*).

These two spiritual giants spent the night poring over sacred texts in order to clarify the permanent location of the Sanctuary. Their deliberations brought them to the conclusion, based upon verses in the Book of Joshua, that the Temple's location must be on the border between the tribes of Judah and Benjamin—in Jerusalem. Jerusalem, then, was to be the "site that God will choose" as home to the Holy Temple (see Deut. 26:2).

David's First Attempt to Bring the Ark of the Covenant to Jerusalem

Upon ascending the throne, David began preparations to build the Temple. His first step was to bring the ark up from Kiriath-jearim to Jerusalem. This he did with great ceremony: "David and the entire House of Israel played before the Lord with all sorts of cypress-wood instruments, with harps, lyres, timbrels, shakers, and cymbals" (2 Sam. 6:5).

A fatal mistake, however, was made at this time. When the oxen pulling the cart stumbled, "Uzzah," says the verse, "reached out and took hold of the ark of God . . . and God smote him there for his error." The *Midrash* elaborates that the source of this calamity was the fact that the ark had been transported by cart. It should have been carried on the shoulders of priests and Levites as it had been in the Wilderness.

King David Brings the Ark to Jerusalem

Seeing the Divine blessing reaped by Obed-edom's household as a result of the ark's presence in their home, David decided to gather the people and bring the ark up to Jerusalem "with shouting and with the sound of the *shofar*. As the ark of the Lord came into the city of David, Michal, Saul's daughter, looked through a window and saw King David dancing and leaping before the Lord . . ." (2 Sam. 6:15–16).

The ark had reached Jerusalem; the Divine services, however, continued to be performed in Gibeon.

z.SMEKhov

King David Declares as Permanent the Altar on Mount Moriah

Together with the prophet Samuel, King David clarified and established the spot where the Temple was to be built—Mount Moriah. Here on Mount Moriah, where Abraham bound Isaac, David built an altar on the threshing floor which he purchased from Ornan the Jebusite. Through this act, he effectively laid the foundations for the Holy Temple in Jerusalem.

Here, David is seen presenting an offering in response to the famine which had befallen Israel. "And the Lord answered him from heaven by fire upon the altar . . ." (1 Chr. 21:26). Ornan the Jebusite and his children stand looking on (to the right).

King Solomon's Prayer at the Dedication of the First Temple

In this illustration, King Solomon concludes his prayer at the dedication of the First Temple. He asks that "whatever prayer and whatever supplication is made by any man of all Your people Israel . . . with hands spread toward this house . . . hear, in Your dwelling place, and forgive, and do, and give to every man according to his ways. . . . Moreover, concerning a stranger, that is not of Your people Israel . . . when he shall come and pray towards this house, hear . . . and do according to all that the stranger calls to You for . . ." (1 Kgs. ch. 8).

Fire miraculously descended from heaven and fell upon the altar. At right, we see the priests bringing the Ark of the Covenant to its resting place within the Holy of Holies. At left is the famed "brazen sea" constructed by King Solomon.

King Solomon's Temple

The First Temple, built by King Solomon, quickly became one of the wonders of the world. This illustration provides us with a view of the Temple Courtyard, featuring the huge "brazen sea," the bronze reservoir that sat upon twelve bronze oxen which Solomon constructed for purification purposes. Special carts used for transporting lavers around the Temple can also be seen, as can the twin pillars, Yachin and Boaz, standing at the entrance to the Sanctuary.

The Interior of the Sanctuary in Solomon's Temple

Solomon's Temple was similar to the Tabernacle in the desert in its basic layout and design, only on a larger scale. Solomon increased the number of sacred vessels in use, according to the needs of Israel and the enlarged size of the Temple. The Sanctuary itself contained not one menorah and one showbread table, but ten of each. The golden candelabra stood on the southern side, the showbread tables on the north, and the incense altar in the center.

Z.SMEKHOV

The Holy of Holies in Solomon's Temple

In King Solomon's Temple, the Ark of the Covenant stood upon the Foundation Stone in the Holy of Holies. According to biblical tradition, this stone is the very center and foundation of all creation.

This ark, constructed of pure gold, contained the original Tablets of the Law which Moses received from God on Mount Sinai. On the Day of Atonement, the High Priest would enter into the Holy of Holies carrying the incense and the coals. Here, he is shown approaching the ark between its two poles.

Towards the end of the First Temple, the ark was removed on the orders of King Josiah and hidden in a spot where, according to Jewish tradition, it remains to this day.

Destruction of the First Temple by King Nebuchadnezzar

Solomon's Temple had lasted 410 years and witnessed the passing of twenty generations of kings from the house of David. All this was put to an end by Nebuchadnezzar when he destroyed the city and exiled the Jews to Babylon together with a portion of the Temple vessels. But even in exile, the people did not lose hope; the nation remained poised and ready for the renewal of the Divine service—in the Second Temple.

The Feast of King Ahasuerus

In the Book of Esther, it is written that King Ahasuerus held a lavish pagan banquet, "and gave them drink in vessels of gold" (Esth. 1:7). According to our sages, these "vessels of gold" were none other than the sacred vessels of the Holy Temple that were plundered from Jerusalem at the time of the destruction.

The Jews Fast and Study the Laws of Passover

In response to the royal decree to exterminate the Jews, Queen Esther told her people to fast for three days and three nights. These three days were during Passover. While fasting, the Jews gathered together to study the laws of the Festival as they had been practiced in Jerusalem's Holy Temple. As Mordecai lectured his distraught people on the intricate laws of the *Omer* barley offering, and the exiles repented their iniquity, Haman arrived with the king's horse and royal robes to accord honor to Mordecai.

Constructing the Altar of the Second Temple

At the completion of the Babylonian exile, a small group of exiles returned to Jerusalem—only to find that the city and the Temple itself still lay in ruins. Nevertheless, they immediately set about constructing the altar in order to resume the sacrificial service.

At that time, the returning exiles "gave money to the hewers and to the carpenters; and food, and drink, and oil, to those in Sidon and Tyre, to bring cedar trees from Lebanon to the sea of Joppa" for the purpose of rebuilding the Temple (Ez. 3:7).

Z. SMEKHOV

The Daily Offering Is Reinstated in the Second Temple

Fifty-two years after the first destruction, the Temple service was renewed. The walls of Jerusalem, its houses, and even the Holy Temple itself still lay in ruins—but the service of the daily offering was reinstated.

Yet, while the younger generation cried for joy at the opportunity to rebuild the Holy Temple, the elders, who remembered the splendor and glory of the First Temple, wept bitterly. Thus, as we see in this illustration, sounds of joy were mixed with the wailing of those who remembered the Presence of God in Solomon's Temple.

Haggai Rebukes the Returnees for Not Building the Temple

Though eighteen years passed since the reinstatement of the daily sacrifice, the Sanctuary remained in a state of ruin. Here, the prophet Haggai rebukes the returnees, calling upon them to shake off their listlessness and to complete the restoration of the Temple which had begun so many years earlier.

Haggai's call was heard: "And the Lord stirred the spirit of Zerubbabel the son of Shealtiel, governor of Judah, and the spirit of Joshua the son of Jehozadak, the High Priest, and the spirit of the remnant of the people; and they came and worked in the House of the Lord of Hosts, their God" (Hag. 1:14).

Here, Zerubbabel and Joshua are seen at right.

Dedication of the Walls of Jerusalem

This illustration portrays the dedication of Jerusalem's walls in the time of the prophets Ezra and Nehemiah. Nehemiah himself informs us that "the wall was finished on the twenty-fifth day of the month of Elul, in fifty-two days. And it came to pass that when all our enemies received word of this, all of the nations surrounding us were afraid...for they perceived that this was the work of God" (Neh. 6:15–16).

Here, we see the traditional joyous procession of the dedication ceremony. The parade is headed by two priests carrying thanks-offerings of leavened bread followed by members of the rabbinical court.

The Hasmonean Priests Light the Menorah After Victory

When the Hasmonean priests rededicated the Holy Temple after it had been defiled by the Greek invaders, they were unable to rekindle the golden menorah—it had been plundered by the enemy. Therefore, they made a simple menorah of seven metal poles. This they lit to fulfill God's commandment to kindle the menorah in the Sanctuary, until they were able to reconstruct the menorah of gold.

Lighting the Menorah from the Sanctuary Courtyard

The *Al Hanissim* prayer recited on Hanukkah recounts, "Your children kindled lights in the Sanctuary Courtyard." Though Jewish law prohibits anybody other than a priest from entering the Sanctuary itself, it permits non-priests to kindle the lights of the menorah from the Sanctuary Courtyard. The priest could bring a menorah candle out to the Courtyard to be lit by an Israelite and then return to the Sanctuary to attach the candle again to the menorah.

Herod's Temple

Here is a bird's-eye view of Herod's Temple, seen from the east.

In contrast to the First Temple built by King Solomon, the appearance of the Second Temple was initially far less impressive. It was built in stages. The initial labor was done by the returning exiles from Babylon; they, though, lacked the means necessary to achieve a majestic result.

In King Herod's time, the Second Temple reached the height of its splendor. He mobilized a multitude of workers and prepared thousands of wagons for transporting wood and dragging gigantic stones. Large numbers of craftsmen and artisans were also trained for this purpose. The sages of Israel lavishly praised it, saying, "Whoever has not seen Herod's building—has never seen a beautiful building in his life."

The Destruction of the Second Temple

The Holy Temple is engulfed in flames as the Roman soldiers mount their attack. The priests, gathered together atop the altar (center), continue with the service and raise their hands to heaven in prayer. Roman soldiers plunder the various golden vessels from the holy Sanctuary. The menorah is led out at the head of the procession, followed by the showbread table and the incense altar. The vessels are thus taken out to exile, together with Israel.

Jewish Sages Frequent the Temple Ruins

Despite a Roman decree prohibiting Jewish settlement in Jerusalem, Jews continued to journey to the site of the Temple after the city's demise. The Talmud tells us how Rabbi Akiva and several of his colleagues went up to Jerusalem. "When they reached Mount Scopus and the site of the Temple came into view, they tore their garments in mourning." Here, pilgrims standing above the ruins behold what had been the Holy of Holies and pray for the Temple's restoration.

The Temple's Timeless Blueprint

When viewing the following illustrations and considering the structure of the Temple and its furnishings, an important principle should be given consideration—uniformity. In structure and in form, the Tabernacle and the First, Second, and Third Temples are all bound by a single unifying thread.

Maimonides informs us that biblical commandments and all of their details are eternally incumbent upon Jews. The Holy Temple is no exception; its various elements do not lend themselves to change. Accordingly, the design of God's Sanctuary must necessarily be homogeneous for any Holy Temple erected by the nation of Israel at any time in history.

An uneducated eye, however, is likely to be struck by numerous, seeming dissimilarities between the structures of the Tabernacle and the First Temple. Indeed, this mistake is likely to repeat itself with the First and Second, as well as the Second and Third Temples. One might reach the erroneous conclusion that each Sanctuary had a structure of its own, a life of its own, independent and unrelated to that of the other Temples.

In truth, though, the essential scheme of God's Holy Temple is eternal and unchanging. The alterations which are discernible from Temple to Temple only affected the cosmetic, outer layers of this undying edifice. In his *Introduction to the Mishnah*, Maimonides points out that it is permitted to enlarge the Temple so long as its basic structure is maintained, "for the relative proportions of its design are Divinely ordained. It is hence written, 'All this is put in writing by the hand of the Lord who instructed me'" (1 Chr. 28:19).

According to an ancient Jewish source, when God gave the Law to Moses on Mount Sinai, He also presented him with a scroll containing instructions of the Temple's layout. Before Moses died, he passed this scroll on to Joshua. Joshua handed it down to the Elders, and so forth, until it reached Samuel the Prophet and King David. King Solomon referred to the guidelines of this scroll when he built the First Temple. The Second Temple, in turn, was built according to the same exact measurements as the First Temple.

Though the Temple Scroll actually contained instructions relevant to the Tabernacle, Solomon was able to apply its principles to the Holy Temple in Jerusalem. These two structures were in fact identical in all aspects but one: the Tabernacle was a portable structure; the Temple was permanent. For example, while the area inside the Tabernacle's Holy of Holies was ten square cubits, in the Temple it was twenty square cubits. The Temple in Jerusalem, then, was twice the size of that in the desert.

So, we can see that while certain aspects of the Temple were altered, the Temple essentially never changed. Its basic structure and proportions remained constant.

Modifications are also discernible in the furnishings of the different Temples. Let us take as an example the bronze basin of water in the Temple's Courtyard. So long as the Children of Israel journeyed through the wilderness, a relatively small laver was sufficient for the needs of the Tabernacle; it held enough water for the four priests who carried out the Divine service at that time: Aaron, Eleazar, Ithamar, and Pinchas. By contrast, King Solomon had *ten* bronze basins constructed for use in the First Temple. He even introduced carts on wheels to ferry these lavers from place to place. Later, in the days of the Second Temple, a special basin was made with twelve faucets from which twelve priests could simultaneously purify their hands and feet before beginning their service in the Temple.

Not surprisingly, the bronze laver which was created by Moses for the four priests serving in the Tabernacle was hardly appropriate for the thousands of priests who worked on a rotating basis of twenty-four watches in the First Temple. It follows that the relative enlargement and development of the Temple and its vessels was an unavoidable phenomenon.

The necessary conclusion as far as the Third Temple is concerned is that it will be built according to the design of the Second Temple, which, in turn, was built according to the blueprint of King Solomon's Temple. We once again refer to Maimonides who explains why the sages troubled themselves composing the mishnaic tract of *Middot*, which appears to be little more than a "story" of the Second Temple. "Its purpose," he writes, "is to provide us with an example of how to build the third Temple." Hence, when he compiled his *Laws of the Temple*, Maimonides incorporated the entire text of tractate *Middot* into his own work. It is clear, then, that the design for the Temple which the Jewish people have been entrusted to build is that which existed in the time of the Second Temple.

This said, the reader will not be surprised to find that the following illustrations all depict the Temple according to the description of the Mishnah. The same is true regarding the Temple's vessels; they appear here as they did in the past, for, as King Solomon himself writes, "That which was is that which will be, and that which has been done is that which shall be done, for there is nothing new under the sun" (Eccl. 1:9).

The Holy Temple

Here is a model of the Second Temple showing its Sanctuary, courtyards, and many chambers. The Holy Temple represents the apex of all human longing: the ability of man to engage in a direct relationship with God. The world awaits the day when the Temple in Jerusalem will once again be the global center of spiritual values. At this one spot on Earth, unlike any other, it will be revealed to all that "God is One and His Name is One" (Zech. 14:9).

The Temple's two main courtyards are the Women's Court, which housed four corner chambers (in foreground), and the Sanctuary Court, beyond the brass Nicanor Gates.

High and Superior Courts in the Temple

The Temple was home to three separate Sanhedrins—two of them Superior Courts consisting of twenty-three sages each, and one a High Court made up of seventy-one judges. The lesser of the two Superior Courts was located north of the entrance to the Temple Mount (bottom right), while the greater was situated just behind it, to the right of the Temple's entrance. The High Court, known as the Great Sanhedrin, sat in the Chamber of Hewn Stone, in the northeast corner of the Temple Courtyard. From here, Torah knowledge, wisdom, and teaching went forth to all Israel, as it is written: "Out of Zion shall go forth Torah, and the word of God from Jerusalem" (Isa. 2:3).

The Gate of Nicanor

The main entrance to the Temple Courtyard was the Nicanor Gate in the east. It was named after the man who donated its doors, and it was the only bronze gate in the Temple. To its right was the Chamber of Pinchas, where priestly vestments were kept; to its left, the Havitin Chamber, where meal-offerings were prepared. There were two smaller gates at each side of the Nicanor Gate and fifteen steps leading down into the Women's Court. This stairway was apparently of a circular shape. The Levites used it as their platform for performing music on certain festive occasions. These stairs were flanked at their base by two chambers in which the Levites kept their musical instruments.

A Golden Vine Above the Sanctuary Gate

Above the entrance to the Sanctuary hung a golden grapevine. This ornament dangled upon the beams of the Sanctuary's Entrance Hall like a real vine. When donations of gold were made to the Temple in the form of grapes or grape leaves, they would be hung here by a priest. From time to time, this vine was removed and its gold was sold for Temple purposes. In the Mishnah, R. Eliezer reports in the name of R. Tzaddok that because of the golden vine's tremendous weight, scores of priests had to be recruited in order to remove it.

The Temple Abattoir

Before animals could be offered upon the Temple's altar, they had to be slaughtered in the Sanctuary Courtyard. To the north of the altar was a special area designated for this purpose. Closest to the altar were twenty-four metal rings which were used to secure the animals; north of these rings were eight small stone columns and eight marble tables. Animals were hung from these columns by hooks before being flayed; the tables were used for rinsing sacrificial organs.

The Chamber of the Seals

The Chamber of the Hearth contained four corner chambers. One of these was the Chamber of the Seals in its northeastern corner. When a person wished to offer a sacrifice, he would first go to this chamber, pay the officiating treasurer the price of the offering, and receive the appropriate clay stamp. The visitor would then use this stamp to purchase his offering.

In addition, it was in this chamber that the Hasmoneans chose to store the stones of the altar (center) which had been desecrated by the idolatrous practices of the Greek kings.

The Chamber of the Lepers

In the northwest corner of the Women's Court was a chamber with a ritual bath for purifying lepers. A leper would immerse here on the eighth day of his cleansing. He would then climb the stairs to the Gate of Nicanor where, with the aid of a priest, he completed the purification process. This bath was also used at times by priests and Israelites who wished to purify themselves before entering the Sanctuary Courtyard.

Chambers for Sacrifice Preparation In the southeastern corner of the Temple Courtyard were three chambers dedicated to the preperation of sacrifices: the Salt Chamber (partially hidden behind the pillar), where salt for the sacrifices was stored; the Parvah Chamber (the door to the right), where the hides were salted; and the Rinsing Chamber (farther right), where the organs of sacrifices were washed.

The Chamber of the Nazirites

Upon completing his vow, a Nazirite travels to the Temple where he must offer sacrifices and shave off his hair. The Mishnah (*Middot* 2:4) tells us that the Chamber of the Nazirites was in the southeastern corner of the Women's Court. "Here, Nazirites would cook their peace-offerings, and shave off their hair and burn it beneath the pot." A special portion of the peace-offering was given to the priest.

Lowering Craftsmen into the Holy of Holies

When repairs had to be made in the Holy of Holies, skilled craftsmen were lowered in boxes through openings in the floor of the Sanctuary's loft. The reason for this practice was, in the words of the Mishnah, "so that their eyes not feast upon the Chamber of the Holy of Holies."

Behind the Holy of Holies

There was a distance of eleven cubits between the western wall of the Sanctuary and the wall of the Courtyard directly behind it. This area was referred to as "the place behind the Chamber of the Ark Cover"—i.e., behind the Holy of Holies. The Talmud informs us that though this area was a good distance from the Israelites' Courtyard in the east, worshipers would prostrate themselves here on Pilgrim Festivals.

The Cells Surrounding the Sanctuary

The Sanctuary was surrounded by thirty-eight cells within the structure's northern, western, and southern walls. The northern and southern walls each contained three levels of five cells each, for a total of thirty. The eastern wall contained two levels of three cells each and another level of two cells, for a total of eight. This computerized depiction gives us an idea of what these cells might have looked like.

The Cell Leading to the Sanctuary Gate

There was a small door to the north of the Sanctuary Gate which opened into a passage leading to a special cell. This cell had five openings, one of which led south into the Sanctuary itself. Each morning, a priest would follow this route to reach the "Great Gate" of the Sanctuary from the inside. He would then unlock the gate and open it wide. This computerized image affords us a view of the passage leading into the Sanctuary.

A View of the Sanctuary's Entrance Hall

This depiction of the Sanctuary's Entrance Hall reveals its inner structure and content: the curtain of the Sanctuary Gate; a marble table upon which the showbread rested before being brought into the Sanctuary; a golden table upon which the loaves were placed when they came out of the Sanctuary; supportive beams stretching from the upper wall of the Sanctuary to that of the Entrance Hall; large golden chains which young priests would climb in order to get a glimpse of the golden crowns that were stored above; the beautiful golden lamp donated by Queen Helena; a golden vine full of golden leaves and grapes which generous people donated to the Temple. Also visible is the opening to the Chamber of the Knives. This was where the priestly watches stored their slaughtering knives.

The Ark of the Covenant

The Bible gives exacting instructions for the construction of the ark, its cover, and the two cherubim (see Exodus 25:10–22). The Tablets of the Law which Moses brought down from Mount Sinai were placed inside the ark, and the ark was housed inside the Holy of Holies. Only the High Priest would enter there, and only on the holiest day of the year, the Day of Atonement. Pictured here is a model of the ark on display at the Temple Institute.

Vessel for Cleaning the Menorah

One aspect of the daily service of the menorah required the priests to clean the seven individual cups. A special vessel which included tongs and a brush was utilized for this task. Here is such a vessel.

Oil Pitcher

This pitcher is designated to replenish the oil for the flames of the menorah and was restored according to a design found on an ancient coin from the Second Temple period. This vessel contains a measurement of 3.5 "*log*" (c. 2 liters).

Small Golden Flask

This vessel was used to pour pure olive oil into the menorah. Oil was poured into this flask from the larger oil pitcher (left) which held enough for all seven flames. This small flask was used to replenish the oil of each individual flame. Its contents were sufficient to burn an entire night, even during the longer nights of the winter season.

The Golden Menorah

The detailed and complicated structure of the menorah is recorded in the *Terumah* Torah portion, which deals with the commandments relating to the structure and furnishings of the Tabernacle (see Exodus 25: 31–40). This candelabrum, on display in the Jewish Quarter of Jerusalem's Old City, was constructed by the Temple Institute for use in the Third Temple. It is fit to be kindled in the Holy Temple in accordance with Jewish law, and it is the first golden menorah constructed since the destruction of the Second Temple.

The Golden Table of the Showbread

Within the holy Sanctuary of the Temple, it is a commandment to display twelve loaves of specially baked bread—corresponding to the twelve tribes of Israel—on this table, before the Divine Presence of God. Constructed of wood and overlain with gold, the showbread table weighed several hundred kilograms. The twelve loaves rested one atop another in two groups of six. Golden shelves separated the loaves to prevent the latter from breaking.

The Frankincense Censors for the Showbread Table

In keeping with the biblical commandment, "Place pure frankincense alongside these stacks" (Lev. 24:6), two bowls like the ones displayed here were filled with frankincense and placed next to the two arrangements of showbread on the sacred table in the holy Sanctuary.

The Golden Menorah with Straight Branches

A discrepancy exists regarding the shape of the menorah's branches. Are they rounded, like those found in ancient drawings, or do they rise in straight diagonal fashion, as Maimonides illustrates in his writings? The question is not imperative, since according to all authorities either version is acceptable for use and legally binding in terms of Jewish law. Today, the generally accepted view is that Maimonides' straight-branched menorah was intended solely as a schematic drawing to illustrate several details of the candelabrum, and that the branches of the menorah in the Holy Temple were indeed rounded.

The Incense Chalice

The talmudic tractate *Tamid* describes a special incense vessel like the one shown here. This vessel holds "half a portion" (approx. 200 grams) of the ingredients for the incense offering. It has an ornate cover topped by a small ring-shaped bell that the priest would sound when entering the Sanctuary.

The Golden Incense Altar

It is a positive commandment to offer incense daily, morning and evening, on the incense altar which stood in the middle of the holy Sanctuary of the Temple. The altar had three names: "the altar of incense," "the golden altar," and "the inner altar."

The altar shown here was constructed by the Temple Institute of gold-plated wood. It was made in accordance with all biblical requirements and is ready for use in the Divine service.

A Shovel for the Incense Offering

A shovel like this was employed to remove burning coals from the outer altar where the fire was constantly burning. The priests also used such a shovel to bring these coals into the Sanctuary to the golden altar, where the incense was offered.

The Outer Altar

On the outer altar, there were three arrangements of wood: the "great woodpile" (right), on which offerings were placed; a second arrangement (immediate left), from which coals were taken for burning the incense on the inner altar; and a third (far corner), which was left smoldering constantly. The center of the altar was reserved for a large pile of ash collected from these three arrangements.

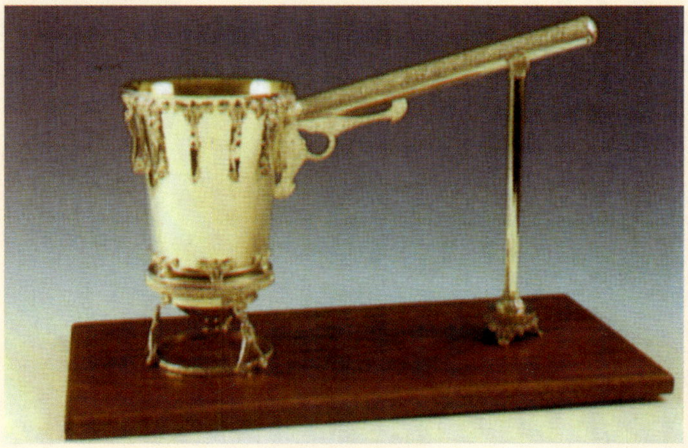

The *Mizrak*

The *mizrak* was one of the sacred vessels used in the Temple service. The priest gathers the blood from the sacrifice into the *mizrak* and then spills it on the corner of the altar. The pointed base prevented the priest from mistakenly setting it down and thereby allowing the blood in it to congeal. A *mizrak* could be of either silver or gold.

A Three-pronged Fork

This kind of fork is mentioned in the Book of Samuel (1 Sam. 2: 12). Authorities like Rashi and Maimonides explain that it was used to turn over the offerings on the altar's fire or to momentarily remove unconsumed portions in order to arrange the altar's large woodpile.

A Measuring Cup

Measuring cups were needed to measure specific amounts of flour, oil, wine, etc., which accompanied, or were ingredients of, the various offerings in the Holy Temple. Here is one such pre-measured vessel.

Meal-offering Vessel

A copper vessel was used to prepare the meal-offering. This offering was comprised of various amounts of flour, oil, and spices.

A Shovel for Removing Ashes

A silver shovel was constantly kept on the southwestern corner of the altar. This shovel was designated for the removal of ashes left on the altar, the very first service done by the priests in the Holy Temple every day, with the first rays of dawn.

Copper Cart

This copper cart was used to remove the excess ashes which accumulated on the altar. It was fashioned with wheels so that it could be maneuvered up the altar's ramp and on the altar itself; chains were attached to it, and two priests would steer the cart to prevent it from tipping over.

The Copper Laver and Stand

Before attending to any duties in the Holy Temple, the officiating priests must sanctify their hands and feet from the water of the laver. The laver was constructed of three distinct parts: the stand; the middle portion, which is the laver itself; and the upper portion, called the *munchi*. The *munchi* was added by a High Priest named Ben-Katin during the Second Temple era in order to circumvent problems of ritual impurity. The laver pictured here, on display at the Temple Institute, features six faucets.

The Silver and Marble Tables

There were two tables to the west of the altar's ramp, one of marble and one of silver. Animal parts from the sacrifices were placed on the marble table while Temple vessels and utensils were put on the silver table. The marble table had an additional function—priests would stand upon it when blowing trumpets to announce the beginning of the daily psalm sung by the Levitical choir.

Stone Vessels for Ritual Purification

Jewish law prescribes that stone vessels be used for preparing the ashes of the red heifer. Here is a collection of such vessels: jugs for drawing water from the Shiloah Spring, containers for preparing the mixture, a mortar and pestle, a vessel for storage, and a bowl used in the sprinkling of the mixture.

Omer Offering Implements

These utensils were used in reaping and preparing the *Omer* offering: a sickle, a basket, and a sieve. There is also a unique apparatus containing a perforated pan above and a receptacle for hot coals below. It was used for roasting the newly ripe barley for the *Omer* offering.

The Lottery and Lottery Box

This is one of the instruments which the High Priest used on Yom Kippur, the Day of Atonement. Lots were drawn to determine which goat would be used as a sacrifice to God, and which would be sent off as an atonement for the sins of the people. During the era of the First Temple, these lots were fashioned of wood; in the time of the Second Temple, they were made of gold. The lots shown here, reproduced by the scholars and craftsmen of the Temple Institute, are constructed of both wood and gold.

The Harp The harp was one of the musical instruments played by the Levites in the Holy Temple. This harp was designed according to an archaeological discovery in the Meggido area. It has twenty-two strings, corresponding to the twenty-two letters of the Hebrew alphabet.

הללוהו בנבל וכינור

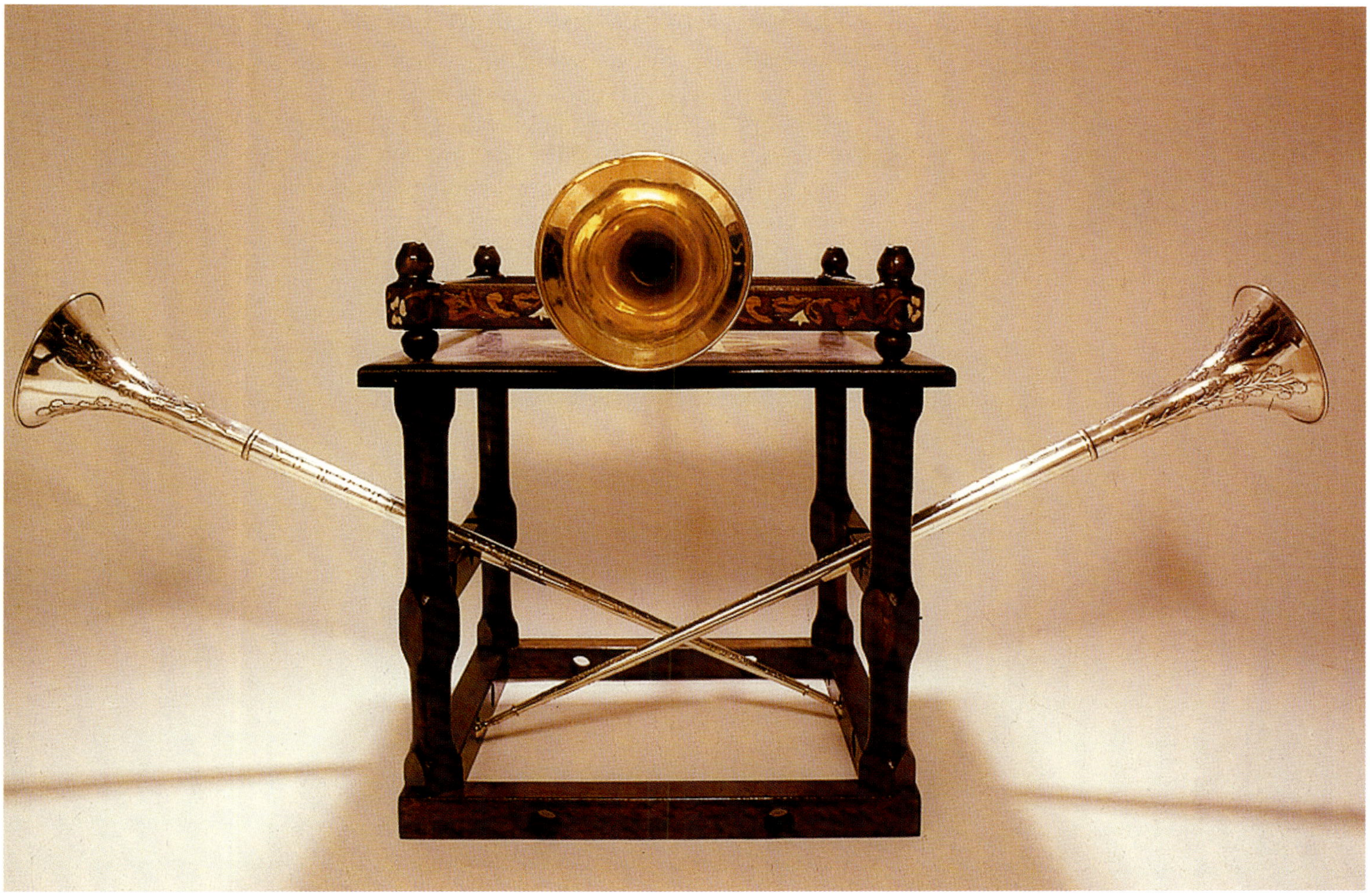

The Silver Trumpets In the Holy Temple, blasts were sounded from the silver trumpets during the sacrificial service, to herald the arrival of the Sabbath, New Month, Festivals, and on other occasions as well. These trumpets have been reconstructed according to Talmudic sources and the Roman Arch of Titus.

The Ram's Horn (*Shofar*)

Gold and silver-plated ram's horns were blown in the Holy Temple. On Rosh Hashanah, a golden *shofar* was blown; on fast-days, a *shofar* of silver was sounded.

The Lyre The lyre played in the Holy Temple had seven strings. According to tradition, the lyre that will be played in the future Temple will feature ten strings, and this is how the instrument has been reproduced. The design of this lyre is based on an ancient coin dating from the Second Temple era. In the Bible, this instrument is also referred to as "the ten-stringed harp." In Jewish tradition, the lyre is associated with King David.

The Uniform of the Ordinary Priests

The ordinary priests wore four garments all year round. These were the same as the "white garments" worn by the High Priest on the Day of Atonement: tunic, pants, hat, and belt. Referring to these priests, the verse states, "And for Aaron's sons you shall make for them tunics, and you shall make for them belts, and you shall make for them hats . . . and make for them linen pants . . ." (Ex. 28:40–42). These garments are to be made from flax, and they must be created from threads consisting of six individual strands.

The Eight Garments

There were eight garments worn by the High Priest throughout the year, in accordance with the biblical verses, "And these are the garments which they shall make: a breastplate, an ephod, a robe and a tunic of checkered pattern, a turban and a belt. And they shall make the sacred garments for your brother Aaron and his sons, to serve me . . . and you shall make a crown of pure gold . . . and make for them linen pants" (Ex. 28:4, 28:36, 28:42).

These garments, when worn during the Temple service, elevated priests to the high levels of sanctity required of those who come to serve before God in the holy place. In addition, the sages teach that the priestly vestments themselves atoned for the sins of Israel.

Wisdom and Understanding

"And you shall speak to all who are wise-hearted, whom I have filled with the spirit of wisdom, that they may make Aaron's garments to consecrate him, that he may minister to me in the priest's office" (Ex. 28:3). From here we learn that the priestly vestments must be made with wisdom and understanding; they must be produced in exact accordance with all the nuances of the biblical requirements. The priestly garments are not sewn, like other clothes. Each item is woven, seamless, of one piece. The only exception to this is the sleeves of the robe, which are woven separately and sewn onto the robe afterwards.

This illustration portrays the High Priest wearing the eight garments as described by Maimonides.

The Priestly Ephod ("Vest") and Breastplate According to Maimonides

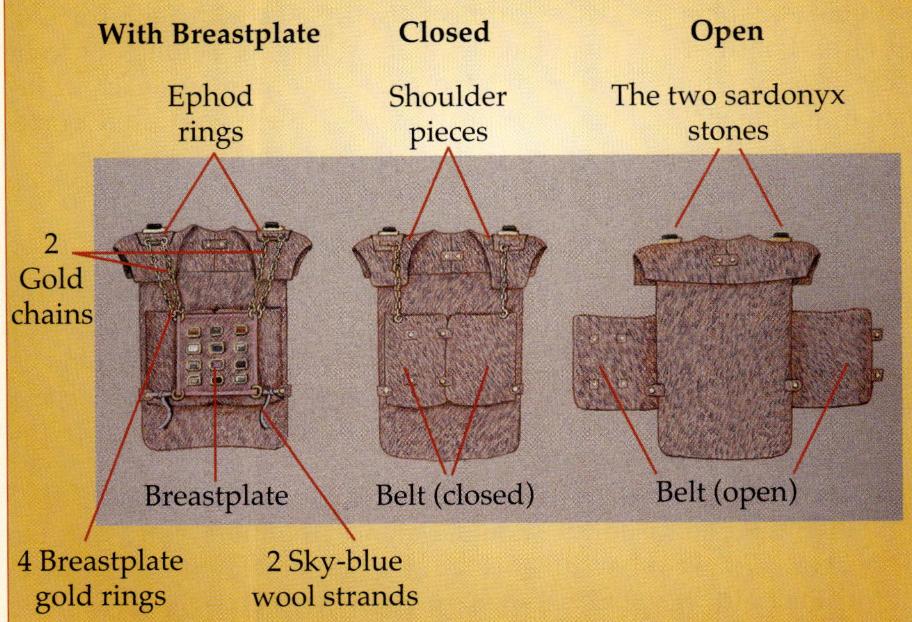

The Two Sardonyx Stones

Two sardonyx stones were fixed in settings of gold on the High Priest's shoulders; one on the right, and one on the left. The names of the tribes of Israel were engraved upon these two stones. The sages explain that when the High Priest entered into the holy place bearing these stones, the Holy One saw all the tribes of Israel inscribed before Him and was moved to have mercy on His people.

The High Priest's Breastplate

"And you shall make the breastplate of judgment, the work of an artist; after the manner of the ephod shall you make it: of gold, sky-blue, dark-red, and crimson dyed wool, and of twisted linen shall you make it" (Ex. 28:6,15). This garment is called a "breastplate of judgment." Square-shaped and worn over the heart, it was so called because of the unique role it played in helping to render fateful decisions.

The garment itself is set with four rows of three small square stones, in settings of knitted or braided gold—one stone for each of the twelve tribes of Israel. The name of the corresponding tribe was engraved on each stone.

The Stones

"And you shall set it with four rows of mounted stones; the first row: a ruby, an emerald, and a topaz. The second row: a carbuncle, a sapphire, and a quartz crystal. The third row: a jacinth, an agate, and an amethyst. The fourth row: a chrysolite, an onyx, and an opal. These stones shall be placed in gold settings. The stones shall contain the names of the twelve Children of Israel, one for each of the twelve stones" (Ex. 28:17–21).

Like the two sardonyx shoulder stones, the Bible states that the purpose of the twelve stones is "to be a perpetual remembrance before the Lord" (Ex. 28:29). When the High Priest bore the breastplate into the holy place, Israel was remembered for peace. The sages taught that it invoked the cause of Israel's salvation and deliverance from her enemies.

The Crown

"And you shall make a crown of pure gold, and engrave on it in the manner of a signet ring: 'Holy to the Lord'" (Ex. 28:36). The crown was a thin plate constructed of one piece of pure, solid gold. Unlike the crown worn by royalty on top of the head, this crown is worn across the forehead and extends from ear to ear. The words "Holy to the Lord" were at times written across two lines, and at times fit into one line.

How the Crown Was Attached

The crown was worn at all times while the High Priest was within the Temple, as the Bible states: "And it shall be worn on Aaron's forehead, that he shall carry the iniquity of the holy things which the Children of Israel shall sanctify in all their holy gifts; and it shall always be upon his forehead, that they may be accepted before the Lord."

The crown had three small holes: two on each end, and one in the center, along the upper edge. Through these holes, threads dyed with sky-blue color were run, and their ends were tied in the back of the priest's head. Thus the crown was kept in place on the High Priest's forehead. In this illustration, however, the priest wears the crown on a special sky-blue woolen cap, as described in the Talmud and other sources.

The Robe

According to most scholars, the robe was a closed garment, seamlessly woven from one piece of fabric, and slipped on over the head. It was worn over the tunic; the tunic was longer than the robe by one handbreadth, so it was visible underneath the robe at the bottom. The opening at the neck was round, with a hem that was doubled over and closed by weaving—not by a needle. The garment hung down in front and in back, and its length extended all the way down to the priest's feet. There is a difference of opinion as to whether there were sleeves. The robe was fashioned exclusively from sky-blue dyed wool, with no other material. The Talmud (*Yoma* 71b) records that its threads were 12-ply.

The Golden Bells

According to the Bible, decorative "pomegranates" made of sky-blue, dark-red and crimson dyed wool were attached to the lower hem of the High Priest's robe together with golden bells. Here is a modern reproduction of the golden bells.

Weaver at Work

Here, a professional weaver intertwines flax filaments to make the thread which will be used for weaving the priestly clothing. The garments of ordinary priests are made from flax, and they must be created from threads consisting of six individual strands.

A Loom

Shown here is a sophisticated hand-driven loom in a workshop for the manufacture of priestly clothing. It presently contains the tunic of the "white garments"—garments worn by the High Priest into the Holy of Holies on the Day of Atonement.

A Distaff

This is a distaff for spinning and twisting wool and flax in preparation for the weaving process. Also visible: a bundle of processed flax ready to be spun and twisted; spools of flax after the twisting process; the "white garments," similar to those worn by ordinary priests in the Temple throughout the year.

The Temple Service: Drawing Near to God

Daily life in Jerusalem's Holy Temple was full of magnificent sights: the torch-lit dawn patrol conducted by the priests; the sounding of the trumpets as the Levitical gate-keepers opened and closed the Temple gates; the kindling of the golden candelabrum and presentation of the incense offering before God; the wine libation on the corner of the altar.

Yet, without a doubt, it was the intricate system of animal sacrifice that occupied the center stage of the Temple's Divine service. A great assortment of sacrifices were offered up in the Temple throughout the year, each type of sacrifice with its own specific laws. For example, there were sin-offerings for the atonement of private individuals, and sin-offerings for the community; peace-offerings brought on Festivals, and peace-offerings brought as voluntary gifts; burnt-offerings for immoral or idolatrous thoughts, and burnt-offerings to accompany other sacrifices. Moreover, the sacrifices were an important element in the larger system of Jewish observance: about 150 of the Bible's total 613 commandments are dedicated to Temple sacrifices. In light of this, it is unfortunate that the Jewish concept of sacrifice as it existed in the Holy Temple is today widely misunderstood.

The significance and meaning of the Temple's sacrificial system is a sensitive and involved subject. It is an issue which deserves—and requires—an entire treatise in its own right. And while this is not the place for a lengthy treatment of the matter, it is worth turning our attention to a number of illuminating points.

If we stop to consider the meaning of the English word "sacrifice," we discover a conceptual gap which may help to account somewhat for the misunderstanding. Sacrifice is commonly defined as "the presentation of an appeasing gift to a deity." In the vernacular, "making a sacrifice" has come to mean renouncing something valued in order to obtain or save something else. The Hebrew term for sacrifice, however, denotes something altogether different. The word is "*korban*." *Korban* is derived from the Hebrew root meaning "to draw near to," or "to establish a close relationship with." And indeed, these expressions convey the essence of the experience which one who offered a sacrifice in the Temple was meant to undergo.

If the definition of *korban* is "to draw near to," then the goal of Temple sacrifice is nothing less than an attempt to elevate human life to a higher sphere of awareness, to draw closer to the ultimate source of life, closer to the Creator. Temple sacrifice does not mean "giving up" or "losing" something of value; it means drawing near to God, for, in the words of King David, "nearness to God is good" (Ps. 73:28). In the eyes of the Jew, being close to God is the truest and most definitive conception of what goodness is. Without this aspect of life to uplift his physical existence and imbue his being with a sense of connection to the Divine, the Jew feels incomplete, empty, devoid of the Divine spark which distinguishes him from the animal.

Nature may be divided into four broad categories: mineral, vegetable, animal, and human. These classes are not only physical, but spiritual as well, for every aspect of the created universe possesses a spiritual essence. Furthermore, these kingdoms are locked in an ongoing struggle with each other; each strives to rise to the next level, and thus become closer to its ultimate source. The sages teach that the only place in the world where these basic forces can achieve harmony and spiritual rectification is in the Holy Temple. As components of the Temple service, these four aspects of creation unite to fulfill God's will and sanctify His name, and in doing this they reach their full potential. The priests who administer the sacrificial service represent humanity; the many sacrifices represent the animal kingdom; the various meal-offerings represent the vegetable kingdom; the salt, which must be a part of every sacrifice, represents the mineral kingdom. Thus, when the Temple stood, all of creation functioned in spiritual harmony. This is one aspect of how the Temple brought peace to the world, as it is written, "...and in this place, I will grant peace, says the Lord of Hosts" (Hag. 2:9).

A View of the Chamber of the Hearth

This large domed chamber served as sleeping quarters for the priests in the Temple. The Chamber of the Hearth was so called on account of the large fire it contained, before which the priests would warm themselves when not on duty. At right, a priest returns the gate key to a special compartment in the floor; at left, an appointed priest knocks on the door to wake his fellow priests.

Chamber of Pinchas, Keeper of Vestments

Priestly garments were stored in this chamber. Upon arrival at the Temple, members of the priestly watch would make their way to this hall and receive the vestments needed for the Divine service. These included tunic, trousers, turban, and sash.

Nighttime Guard Duty in the Temple

In the Temple, there were twenty-four posts at which priests and Levites kept guard throughout the year. The purpose of this watch was to reflect honor upon the Sanctuary, for, in the words of the sages, "[The honor accorded] a palace surrounded by guards is greater than [that accorded] a palace which is left unguarded."

At night, an overseer bearing the title "Man of the Temple Mount" made the rounds of the sentry posts to ensure that the watchmen were on their guard. If he happened to come upon a guard who was dozing, he would beat him with his staff. The overseer even had the right to singe the watchman's garment for sleeping on duty.

The Dawn Patrol

After immersing in a ritual bath, the priests began their torch-lit dawn patrol of the Temple Courtyard. This was carried out on a daily basis in order to assure that each of the sacred vessels needed for the Temple service was in its place. The patrol came to an end by the Havitin Chamber.

Allocating Priests for the Daily Temple Service

A type of balloting was employed in order to choose which priests would participate in the day's Temple service. As we see in this illustration, the priest responsible for assigning the services would remove the turban of one of his associates to indicate that the balloting would begin from him.

Removal of Ashes from the Altar

The priestly service in the Holy Temple began each day with the removal of a small portion of ashes from the previous day's offerings. These ashes were brought down from the altar and poured into a special hole in the floor of the Temple Courtyard adjacent to the altar and to the east.

The Sanctification of Hands and Feet and Preparation of the Altar

After the ashes had been removed from the altar, all priests were required to wash (sanctify) their hands and feet from special faucets in the washbasin of the Temple. Following this, they hurried up the altar to begin preparing the arrangements of wood for the coming day's offerings.

The Chamber of the Wood

One of four large chambers in the Women's Court was the Chamber of the Wood. Situated in the southeast corner of the Courtyard, it served as a storage room for the split wood which was to be burned upon the altar. Before being brought to the altar, each piece was inspected for worms.

Placing Two Logs Upon the Altar

There is a Divine commandment to add two logs of split wood to the altar's fire twice daily—before the morning and afternoon *tamid* offerings. While two separate priests carried the pair of logs brought in the afternoon, those brought in the morning were carried by a single priest.

The Chamber of the Vessels

The Mishnah tells us that each morning the priests would "enter the Chamber of the Vessels and bring out ninety-three vessels of silver and gold" needed for the Divine service (*Tamid* 3:4). Though we find no explicit mention of this chamber's location, it appears to have been situated in the Women's Court.

The Chamber of the Lambs

The Chamber of the Hearth possessed four side chambers, one of which housed the animals that were to be offered up on the altar. Such animals had to be brought four days prior to their being offered so that they could be inspected for disqualifying blemishes. There were never fewer than six acceptable lambs in this chamber at one time.

The First Stage in Opening the Sanctuary

In order to open the large Sanctuary gate it was first necessary to open a smaller door to the north of the gate. This door could only be opened from the inside, and to do this one of the priests had to insert his entire arm through a window in the door and unlock a bolt which was fixed to a socket in the floor.

"Barkai!" The Holy Temple's sacrificial service commenced at daybreak with the slaughtering of the daily *tamid* offering. In this illustration, a watchman is seen standing on a lookout tower gazing to the east. With the first rays of sun he shouts, *"Barkai!"* ("Morning has arrived!"). This was the indication that the Divine service could begin.

Z. SMEKHOV

Priests Enter the Sanctuary, Levites Mount Their Platform

While the *tamid* was being offered up, one of the priests would "take a gong and throw it between the Entrance Hall and the altar . . ." (*Tamid* 5:6). The Mishnah goes on to tell us that priests who heard the sound of this gong would run to join their associate priests prostrating themselves in the Sanctuary; Levites would hurry to join the other Levites in song on the platform.

The Opening of the Sanctuary Gate

Here, a priest opens wide the large Gate of the Sanctuary from inside. This was the signal to his colleague in the Courtyard to begin slaughtering the morning *tamid* offering. The slaughterer did so with his back to the east in order to repudiate the practices of the sun-worshipers. The opening of this large gate, it was said, could be heard as far as Jericho.

The Essential Steps of the Offerings

Every sacrificial offering included four indispensable actions: slaughter; receiving the blood; carrying it to the altar; and sprinkling it thereupon. The priest on the right is carrying the blood to the altar; the other two are busy sprinkling it. Depending on the offering, sprinkling could mean dashing the blood on the corner of the altar or pouring it on the base.

Bringing the *Tamid* to the Altar

In this illustration, we see the procession of priests that would bring the parts of the *tamid* to the altar. They also brought meal mixed with oil for the meal-offering and wine for the libations, both of which were offered each day with the morning and afternoon *tamid* offerings.

The Throwing of the Offering Parts

The parts of the daily offering were thrown from the top of the altar's ramp into the large arrangement of wood on the altar's southeast corner. In this depiction, we see one priest (left) about to perform the wine libation, and another (second from left) presenting the meal-offering.

Recitation of the *Shema* on the Mount of Olives

When sunlight reached the Sanctuary's entrance, the people of Jerusalem knew that the time had come to recite the morning prayers. In this illustration, we view the Holy Temple from the Mount of Olives. As the first rays of sunlight reach the entrance of the Sanctuary, those working in the area cease their labors and recite the *Shema* prayer, a proclamation of faith in the one true God.

Queen Helena's Lamp

In the Second Temple, a beautiful golden ornament, a lamp donated by Queen Helena, hung over the Sanctuary entrance. The sages relate that every morning as the sun began to rise over Jerusalem, the rays of sunlight would strike this golden lamp and the bright light reflected off of it could be seen all over the city. Thus, the citizens knew that it was time to recite the *Shema* prayers.

Daniel Kneels in Prayer Toward Jerusalem

Daniel the Prophet kneels in prayer with his hands extended heavenward. From Daniel's manner of prayer, the sages of Israel understood the act of kneeling to be a form of worship before God.

Kneeling

The proper manner of kneeling is learned from King Solomon, of whom we are told, "And he went down upon his knees before the entire congregation of Israel and extended his hands toward heaven" (2 Chr. 6:12).

Jewish tradition provides clear guidelines for correct prostration. This painting illustrates the first three stages (right to left): falling to the knees, sitting in a kneeled position, and bowing down while still in a kneeled position.

The "Kneeling Stone" in the Temple

Though the Bible (Lev. 26:1) teaches that prostration upon a decorated stone is forbidden, it was permitted in the Temple. Here, father and son kneel on one such stone before the outer fence of the Temple Courtyard. When the Greeks invaded the Sanctuary, they broke through this fence in thirteen places—a proclamation that the prohibition against Gentile entry into the Temple was null and void. Later, when the Hasmonean priests prevailed and retook the Temple, they decreed that all who visit the holy site should prostrate themselves opposite these breaches.

The Daily *Tamid* Offering in the Temple

Here is a view of the inner court of the Holy Temple during the service of the daily sacrifice. At left, the Levitical choir stands atop the platform and provides musical accompaniment; in the center stands the altar, the Sanctuary rising up behind it; at right, the area where the offering parts are prepared for the altar.

The Priests at Prayer in the Chamber of Hewn Stone

In the middle of the daily morning service, the priests would assemble in the Chamber of Hewn Stone in order to recite the *Shema*: "Hear, O Israel, the Lord is our God, the Lord is One" (Deut. 6:4). This would begin with the one in charge saying, "Recite one blessing." The priests would also recite the Ten Commandments at this time.

Attending to the Menorah

Every morning, a priest would attend to the seven-branched candelabrum in the Sanctuary. This regular priestly duty included cleaning out the menorah, replacing and relighting the wicks, and replenishing the olive oil. The menorah symbolized the light which the Temple radiates to the world.

Offering the Incense

The *Zohar* teaches that the incense-offering was the most beloved part of the Temple service in God's eyes. This twice-daily service required the participation of three priests. When the incense was finally scattered over the coals, a straight column of smoke rose up to the ceiling, spreading out and filling the entire Sanctuary.

The Chamber of the Oils

Located in the southwest corner of the Women's Court, the Chamber of the Oils was where the oil for the meal-offerings, the menorah, and other Temple lamps were kept. It also contained casks of wine needed for the libations. This chamber, like the other three corner chambers in the Women's Court, was unroofed.

The Priestly Blessing

With the conclusion of the morning service, the priests would stand on the steps of the Sanctuary and bless the people with the Priestly Blessing. As in our illustration, the five priests who had cleared the ashes from the inner altar and the menorah would "stand to the south of their fellow priests holding five vessels," while the other priests lifted their hands according to the traditional rite and pronounced the benediction as it appears in Numbers 6:24-26: "May God bless and protect you…." The High Priest (left) was careful not to raise his hands higher than his forehead plate (*Tamid* 7:2).

The Levitical Choir

As the designated priest prepared to pour the wine libation (far left), the assistant High Priest would wave a kerchief, signaling his colleagues below to sound the cymbals and blow the trumpets. The Levites would play the harps and the lyres and begin to sing a psalm. When they came to a break in the psalm, the trumpets were sounded and the people would prostrate themselves toward the Holy of Holies.

Thus, the Levites accompanied the Divine service of the priests with a service of their own. They complemented each other. In many ways, the Levitical songs were as important as the priestly service of the offerings, for one could not function without the other.

The Sabbath *Mussaf* Offering and Showbread Replacement

In addition to the daily *tamid* offering, the Sabbath day saw both the arrangement of new loaves on the table of the showbread, and the bringing of the *mussaf* additional Sabbath offering. This illustration captures the priests bringing both the lambs for the *mussaf* offering and the new showbread.

Trumpets Blown to Herald the Sabbath

In the Holy Temple, blasts were sounded from silver trumpets to herald the arrival of the Sabbath. With the approach of the hallowed day of rest, six blasts were blown: "Three, to cause the masses to cease their labor, and three, to announce the transition from the mundane to the sacred" (*Sukkah* 53b).

Changing of the Breads in the Sanctuary

On Sabbath, four pairs of priests entered the Sanctuary: two pairs to replace the showbread and two pairs to replace the golden censors of frankincense. In this manner, not even a moment passed when the breads were not in their proper place on the table, as the biblical commandment requires. Tradition relates that a miracle constantly occurred: when the previous week's loaves were removed, they were found to be fresh and warm, as if they had just come out of the oven.

Breastplate Consultation According to Rashi

According to Rashi, consultation with the breastplate did not take place in the Sanctuary before the ark. Rather, the king and the High Priest would stand facing each other while the question was asked. In this depiction, the king (right) wishes to know if the Nation of Israel should go to war.

Consulting the Breastplate in the Holy of Holies

In times of war and other unusual circumstances, the High Priest and king would enter the Sanctuary and ask the community's question before the Presence of God. The High Priest would then meditate on the stones of the breastplate and receive his answer through certain letters on the stones which would shine in a special manner. This oracle was used until the destruction of the First Temple.

The Chamber of Hewn Stone

One of the larger chambers in the Holy Temple was the Chamber of Hewn Stone. Constructed of great, finely crafted stones, it was likened to "a sort of great basilica." It was within this chamber, located in the Temple Courtyard near the altar, that the members of the Sanhedrin sat in judgment. Hence, the Holy Temple was both a source of Torah wisdom and a place of Divine service.

The Great Sanhedrin was Israel's Supreme Court and highest body of legislation, justice, and wisdom. Its president carried on and passed down the traditions that were received directly from Moses at Mount Sinai. As noted, the Sanhedrin convened in the Chamber of Hewn Stone, a large hall built into the Temple's north wall, half inside the Sanctuary area and half outside. Court members sat in a semicircle headed by the president and his deputy, while opposite this body sat students of law. Here, litigants present their case before the court.

The Sanhedrin's Semicircle According to Maimonides

Rabbi Moses Maimonides, the Rambam, was of the opinion that it was not students but members of the Sanhedrin who sat opposite the president and his deputy. Facing them, as they did, in a semicircle, the sages of the Sanhedrin were more accurately able to follow the judicial rulings of these two revered sages.

Women in the Service of God

When one considers the many aspects of the Temple's Divine service, questions automatically arise concerning the place of women in the Temple. What was *their* role? How were *they* involved in the sacrifices, prayers, and other elements of the Divine service?

Let us begin to answer this question by going back to the very inception of the Sanctuary institution—the desert Tabernacle. We find that when God commanded the Children of Israel to "build Me a Sanctuary, and I will dwell among them" (Ex. 24:8), it was the women who were quickest to act. The women of Israel were the first to bring donations for the construction of the Tabernacle in the wilderness. How do we know this? In describing the manner in which the Children of Israel came forth to make their donations, Scripture tells us that "the men came along with the women" (ibid. 35:22). The sages of the *Midrash* comment: "From here we learn that the women preceded the men in bringing their donations." The great medieval Bible commentator, Nahmanides, explains that as soon as the opportunity offered itself, the women removed their jewelry and hurried to bring it as a donation for the Tabernacle. The *Midrash* further explains that in reward for their enthusiastic generosity, the women of that generation merited entering the Land of Israel, while the men did not.

At the very outset, then, we discover women playing a definitive role in the establishment of the Sanctuary and in creating a fitting abode for the Divine Presence in Israel's midst. Their generous behavior evinced an intense faith in God—a faith that was to leave an indelible impression upon the Jewish people for all generations.

If we take a closer look at the various elements and obligations of the Temple service, it becomes evident that women were granted considerable freedom and opportunity. They played an active role in much of what went on there throughout the year, and they were able to do this in a manner that befitted both their femininity and their family responsibilities.

Already in Moses' day, arrangements were made so that women would be able to worship freely in the Tabernacle Courtyard. The opening chapter of the Book of First Samuel teaches us that this was also the case when Eli served as High Priest in the Shilo Sanctuary. In the First Temple, during the reign of King Jehoshaphat, a new courtyard was added to the Temple complex. The "Women's Court," as it would become known, was the largest and most visited of the Temple's courts. It was established as a separate court for the women who would come to pray and offer sacrifices in the Temple. With the Second Temple came another important renovation which benefited the women: the "Women's Gate"—one of the seven grand gates leading into the Sanctuary Court.

One might expect that with a special court of their own, there would be no need for women to enter the exclusive Sanctuary Courtyard. We find, however, that women were no more restricted than men in this regard. Women were permitted to enter the Sanctuary Court, and they would often go there to bring sacrifices, prostrate, offer prayer and confession, voice repentance, and more. Under certain circumstances, women would even enter the Courtyard to slaughter animal sacrifices or perform various wave-offerings.

In addition to the part they played in the Temple's Divine service, women participated in the actual construction of both the Tabernacle and the Holy Temple. Maimonides teaches us that the Biblical precept to build a Temple was incumbent upon both men and women. Moreover, women were employed in special Temple workshops to weave the Temple curtains and the thousands of priestly vestments.

It is clear, then, that women participated in nearly every aspect of the Temple service and were even active in the construction and upkeep of the Temple complex. The following chapter provides many colorful depictions which seek to illustrate the various shades of this intimate relationship—the relationship between the women of Israel and the Holy Temple.

The Women Donate Their Mirrors

Women took an active role in donating goods for the construction of the Tabernacle and its vessels. In fact, the washbasin and its base were made entirely of copper mirrors brought by the women. Initially, Moses was reluctant to receive this gift. "The women use these mirrors," he reasoned, "to beautify themselves in order to attract and arouse men; they are not a fitting ingredient for God's Holy Sanctuary." God, however, ordered Moses to accept them, for it was by virtue of these mirrors that Jewish wives in Egypt succeeded in arousing their husbands and bearing many children despite the relentless bondage.

Hannah Prays in Front of the Sanctuary

"So Hannah arose after they had eaten in Shilo, and after they had drunk, and Eli the priest sat upon a seat by the door-post of the Temple of the Lord; and her soul was embittered, and she prayed unto the Lord and wept terribly" (1 Sam. 1:9).

In this illustration, Hannah is seen standing in prayer between the altar and the Sanctuary. As she leaves, Eli tells her to "go in peace, and the God of Israel will grant your request...."

Jonah's Wife Brings a *Re'iyah* Offering

Though the Torah precept to bring a *re'iyah* burnt-offering to the Temple on each of the Pilgrim Festivals applies to Jewish males, women are permitted to bring such an offering if they so desire. The wife of Jonah the Prophet, for example, would make the arduous journey to Jerusalem to bring a *re'iyah* offering. This was no easy task in those days, for King Jeroboam and his successors outlawed Temple pilgrimages and set up barriers to deter perpetrators.

When a Woman Petitions God for Rain

The Talmud relates how once, during an extended drought, Abba Hilkiyah and his wife went up on their roof and prayed for rain. "Abba Hilkiyah stood in one corner and his wife stood in another, and before long rain clouds rolled in toward where his wife stood." When the sages who witnessed this event asked Abba Hilkiyah why his wife's supplications were so effective, he replied, "My wife is quick to provide food for the needy who come begging; God is therefore quick to provide rain for her when she begs."

"The New Court"

The Second Book of Chronicles (Ch. 20) describes how, as the armies of Moab and Ammon came against Israel in battle, King Jehoshaphat stood on the Temple Mount before a large congregation, "in front of the new court," and asked God to come to His people's aid. This "new court" later became known as the Women's Courtyard, and it was the largest and most visited court in the Temple

The Women's Gate

The Temple had a special gate designated for women coming to offer sacrifices. Here is a view of the Women's Gate (middle) from the north as it appeared during the Passover Festival. To its left is the "Song Gate" through which Levite musicians and singers would enter.

The Women's Gate in the Second Temple

In the Second Temple, women could be seen entering the Women's Gate throughout the year with any of a number of offerings. When bringing a sacrifice, a woman had to be present to witness the slaughter. She accompanied her offering with prayer, confession, repentance, prostration, and praise of God for His abundant kindness. In the case of a Passover sacrifice, if no family member was available to slaughter for her, a woman was obligated to slaughter the lamb herself.

Women Comfort Women on the Temple Mount

The Mishnah teaches that all who entered the Temple Mount would turn right and proceed in that direction until exiting. The exception to this rule were those who had experienced hardships; they proceeded to the left. This arrangement allowed visitors to console the dejected. In this illustration, we see women coming from the right comforting those approaching from the opposite direction.

The Women's Court and Its Four Chambers

Though most rabbinic authorities hold that a large part of the Women's Court was taken up by four corner-chambers, Rabbenu Asher ben Yehiel (1250–1327) is of the opinion that these chambers were situated—as depicted in this illustration—on the *outer* corners of the courtyard. Without a doubt, such an arrangement would have allowed women ample space and freedom to pray and worship God.

Women Perform *Semicha*

In many cases, Jewish law requires a man who brings a sacrifice to the Temple to press both of his hands down on the head of the animal before it is slaughtered — a procedure known as *"semicha."*

According to some opinions, women may perform a similar ceremony if they wish. In this depiction, a priest stands in the Women's Court on the stairs leading to the Sanctuary and waits for women to finish pressing their hands on a sacrifice.

The Childbirth Purification Offering

After giving birth, a woman must offer a childbirth sacrifice in the Temple. This offering comprised a yearling lamb for a burnt-offering and a young pigeon or turtledove for a sin-offering. If the woman cannot afford the cost of the lamb, she can bring two young pigeons or two turtledoves—one as a sin-offering and one as a burnt-offering. Here, women stand in the Nicanor Gate and present their childbirth offerings to the priest.

A Nazirite Woman Brings Her Offerings

A Nazirite vow is one method of achieving spiritual uplift and sanctity, and the Torah gives equal opportunity to men and women in this area. A Nazirite must abstain from consuming anything derived from the vine; avoid contact with the dead; and refrain from cutting his hair. Upon completing his vow, the Nazirite travels to the Temple where he must offer sacrifices and shave off his hair. Here, a Nazirite and Naziritess present their offerings to priests in the Temple Courtyard. Portions of the sacrifices were ceremonially waved by the priests.

Oath of the Suspected Adulteress Chapter 5 of the Book of Numbers describes in lengthy detail the procedure that must be followed in the case of a suspected adulteress ("*sotah*"). In such instances, a husband cannot be intimate with his wife until her fidelity has been established. Part of the ceremony involves the woman's taking an oath at the eastern gate of the Temple Courtyard—the Nicanor Gate—while facing the Holy of Holies. In this portrayal, the suspect, having asserted her innocence, prepares to take her oath.

The Parchment and the Bitter Water

Here, the suspected adulteress is seen holding the special meal-offering she is required to bring to the Temple. Her hair is being uncovered in accordance with the verse, "And the priest shall . . . expose the woman's hair" (Num. 5: 18). At right, a priest prepares a small parchment (he copies its text from a gold wall plaque donated by Queen Helena) that will be submerged in the "bitter water." A third priest is preparing this water for the woman to drink.

Women in the Chamber of the Curtain

One of the jobs in the Temple which was placed in the hands of women was that of weaving the Sanctuary curtains and other curtains hung over certain gates in the Temple complex. In addition to this important responsibility, women made the High Priest's garments as well as the thousands of vestments worn by priests serving in the Temple year-round.

From the Mishnaic tractate *Middot* we learn that weaving was carried out in a special chamber known as the "Chamber of the Curtain." This chamber was guarded on a constant basis, possibly because of the flammable materials employed therein.

Here is an illustration of women at work spinning thread and weaving the Sanctuary curtain. On the right, a woman prepares the sky-blue and dark red dyes needed for the curtain.

Women Bring the Firstfruits

In this illustration, a woman brings a basket of firstfruits and an animal offering to the Temple. While women were bound by the commandment to bring firstfruits to the Courtyard of the Sanctuary between the Festivals of Shavuot and Sukkot, there were certain parts of the ceremony which they did not perform. A woman would carry her basket of fruits on her shoulder into the Courtyard; recite, "I affirm this day ..." (Deut. 26:3); set down the basket by the altar; prostrate before God, and exit.

Women on *Seder* Night

Women were obligated to make the pilgrimage to Jerusalem in order to offer and partake of the Passover sacrifice. Even where the father or husband was for some reason unable to travel to the Temple, the woman was required to go up to the Holy City and fulfill her own personal obligation. Moreover, the sages permitted women to perform their own separate Passover *seder* if they desired.

Preparations for the Fifteenth of Av and Yom Kippur

"Israel knew no holiday comparable to the Fifteenth of Av and Yom Kippur. On these occasions, the young women of Jerusalem would go out with borrowed white clothing . . . to dance circles in the vineyards" (*Bikkurim* 26b). According to the sages, women loaned garments to each other so that one who was lacking would not be embarrassed. Here, women exchange gowns which have been stored away for the occasion.

The Daughters of Shilo Dance in the Vinyards

"Behold, there is a feast to God each year in Shilo, which is to the north of Bethel" (Judg. 21: 19). The sages indicate that this "feast to God" took place on the Fifteenth of Av: "Israel knew no holiday that could compare to the Fifteenth of Av ... the day on which the Tribe of Benjamin was again permitted to marry into the Congregation [of Israel]." In other words, the day on which the men of Benjamin took wives from among the daughters of Shilo dancing in the vineyards (as described in Judges Ch. 21) was the Fifteenth of Av. The joy and celebration which found expression at this time of year in Shilo was probably due to the grape harvest and the firstfruit offering in the Sanctuary which were then at their height. This Festival later spread to Jerusalem.

Women at the Water Libation Celebration

Men, women, and children participated in the immense joy of the water libation—some directly, while others stood and watched. Because these festivities took place in the Women's Court, elevated balconies were constructed, enabling the women to watch the dancing of the wise men of the Sanhedrin from above. The sages referred to the introduction of these balconies, which prevented inadvertent levity, as a "great rectification."

Rachel Laments for Her Children

"Thus says the Lord . . . Rachel is weeping for her children; she refuses to be comforted because they are not. Thus says the Lord, keep your voice from weeping . . . for your children shall come back again to their own border" (Jer. 31:14–16). The sages relate that when the Holy Temple was destroyed and the people of Israel were taken into captivity, the matriarch Rachel came out and cried bitterly over her children's fate as they passed by her tomb on their way to exile. The biblical verses describe Rachel's crying, and God's answer to her.

Rosh Hashanah's Call to Remembrance

Rosh Hashanah is referred to as the "Day of Remembrance." It is also called the "Day of Sounding." We indeed encounter a mixture of these two elements on this day.

Rosh Hashanah is a "Day of Remembrance" because it is acknowledged by Jewish tradition as being the day on which all of humanity is judged. According to the sages, it was on this day that the creation of the world was completed. What more appropriate day of the year could there be for self-examination, repentance, and atonement than the day on which the first human being came into existence.

Jewish tradition relates that Adam himself was judged on the day of his creation. *Pesikta DeRav Kahana* gives the following account of the events which transpired on that fateful day. "It was on Rosh Hashanah that the first human being was created. During the first hour of the day the idea took shape in God's mind; in the second hour, He consulted the ministering angels; in the third, He gathered the necessary dust; in the fourth, He kneaded it; in the fifth, He formed the limbs; in the sixth, He stood the body upright; in the seventh, He infused it with a soul; in the eighth, He placed him in the Garden of Eden; in the ninth, God commanded him; in the tenth, Adam transgressed God's commandment; in the eleventh, he stood in judgment; in the twelfth, he was pardoned by God. The Almighty said, 'Let this be a sign for your offspring. Just as you stood before Me in judgment and were acquitted on this day, so will your children face judgment on this day and be acquitted.'"

This, then, is the meaning of the "Day of Remembrance." It is a day on which each and every being in creation is examined and judged separately. The Mishnah testifies to this when it says (*Rosh Hashanah* 16a), "On Rosh Hashanah, all beings pass before Him like tender sheep." We pass before our Creator one by one like the sheep being counted by the shepherd.

The sages portray Mount Moriah, the location of the Temple, as occupying a center stage in the events of the creation. It was here that the first man was created; here he sinned and repented; here he built an altar and presented an offering.

There is also a tradition that Adam stood on this spot and sanctified the new moon for the first time in history. In this sense, the new moon and the New Year are married by an essential bond: on Rosh Hashanah the moon makes its reappearance. Hence, everything is renewed on the Jewish New Year: the month, the year, and, most important, man. Man is renewed through repentance and good deeds. And all of this is played out on the hallowed Temple Mount.

In the Holy Scriptures, Rosh Hashanah is called a "Day of Sounding." This concept is also connected to the Temple. According to tradition, the Binding of Isaac upon an altar on Mount Moriah took place on this day. The "sounding" which one hears in synagogues all over the world on Rosh Hashanah is blown through a ram's horn in order to remind us of the ram that replaced Isaac as a sacrifice.

The sounding of the ram's horn comes, then, to remind us of two things. First, it takes us back to the very beginning of it all, to the day of the world's inception—to man's fall and repentance. Second, it recalls the Binding of Isaac and the laying of the foundation of the Temple for the Jewish people.

These and other concepts find expression in the following collection of illustrations and their accompanying explanations. The vivid portrayals in this chapter bring us face to face with ideas that go back to Israel's very beginnings—ideas which, because they are so intimately and eternally bound up with the Day of Judgment, allow us to penetrate the true depths of this day.

Rosh Hashanah in the Temple—Repentance for the Returnees

Following the Babylonian exile, Rosh Hashanah commenced a month-long campaign for repentance in the Temple. Ezra and Nehemiah convened the returned exiles in the Temple Courtyard and read to them from a Torah scroll—a ceremony aimed at strengthening the faith and observance of the returnees. Scripture describes the event: "When the seventh month came . . . all of the people gathered together as one man into the open place that was before the Water Gate" (Neh. 7:72–8:1).

When the crowd heard the words of the Torah and grasped the enormity of their sins, they began to wail and lament. Ezra and the Levites, however, calmed the people, proclaiming, "This day is sacred to the Lord! Stop your mourning and your crying!"

Here, Ezra (far left), flanked by Levites, reads from the Torah scroll. At the foot of the wooden platform additional Levites quiet the perturbed congregants. Notice that the color and style of the Temple's architecture reveal a strong Babylonian influence.

Blowing the *Shofar* Before the Sanctuary Gates

On Rosh Hashanah, the *shofar* was blown together with the silver trumpets. In this illustration, three priests stand on the stairs leading up to the Sanctuary, in keeping with the verse, "With trumpets and *shofar* blasts sound off *before the King, God*" (Ps. 98:6). The priest in the middle blows the *shofar* while at his side stand two priests who accompany his *shofar*-blasts with the sound of the trumpet.

The *Rosh Hodesh* (New Moon) Additional Offering on Rosh Hashanah

As soon as witnesses testified to having seen the new moon, and the court announced the onset of both the new month and New Year, the *Rosh Hodesh* offering was presented. It included eleven animals: two young bulls, one ram, seven yearling sheep, and one goat. In the Holy Temple, the first day of the new month was also a day of atonement for Israel. The focal point of the day was the bringing of the goat for a sin offering.

The Rosh Hashanah Additional Offering

Inasmuch as Rosh Hashanah is also the first day of the month of Tishrei, there were many offerings in the Temple on this occasion: the daily sacrifice, that of *Rosh Hodesh* (see above), and the sacrifices for Rosh Hashanah. Comprising ten animals—one young bull, a ram, seven yearling sheep, and a goat—the special Rosh Hashanah offering was brought after that of *Rosh Hodesh*.

Favor for Jerusalem on Rosh Hashanah

The sages granted special status to Jerusalem on Rosh Hashanah: even when the latter fell on the Sabbath, the blowing of the *shofar* was permitted in the Holy City. This was the rule not only within the Temple and on its mount; it applied to the entire city even as far as the surrounding villages. Here is a depiction of one such village. Because it is within seeing and walking distance of Jerusalem, its inhabitants are allowed to blow the *shofar* on the Sabbath.

Shofar and Trumpet Blasts at the Eastern Gate

In addition to the *shofar*-blowing ceremony on the stairs of the Sanctuary, blasts were sounded before the eastern gate of the Temple Mount, as depicted here. This was done so that the ritually impure, who were unable to enter the Temple, would not be denied the opportunity to be part of this unique event. The *shofar* blast in the Holy

Temple was indeed unique, for it was blown together with two trumpets—one on each side. The gold-plated *shofar* sounded long blasts, and the trumpets, short, such that ultimately only the *shofar* would be heard.

Once, When Witnesses Arrived Late…

In the time of the Holy Temple, when the appearance of the new moon was determined through eyewitness testimony, Rosh Hashanah began with some uncertainty. This was due to the fact that it took some time for the witnesses to arrive and give an account of what they had seen. Therefore, the people would begin to observe the holiday as a precautionary measure even before actual new-moon testimony had been given. With the

arrival and testimony of witnesses, the head of the court would announce, "The day is hallowed!" and the day's Temple services would begin.

Once, witnesses arrived just before nightfall. In the ensuing confusion, the Levites failed to sing their daily psalm. In response, the sages ruled that testimony would no longer be accepted after the time of the daily afternoon burnt-offering. If by this time no witnesses had arrived, the following day would be observed as Rosh Hashanah in all respects.

Sanctification of the New Moon on the Sabbath

In Temple times, and as long as the Great Sanhedrin functioned, the month was sanctified through two witnesses who testified that they had seen the new moon. In this manner, it was determined whether the previous month had been an "incomplete" month of twenty-nine days or a "full" month of thirty days. New-moon witnesses were permitted to violate the Sabbath in order to reach Jerusalem while still daytime so that the priests could offer up the additional *Rosh Hodesh* sacrifices. Moreover, even those who had not themselves seen the new moon were allowed to violate the Sabbath in order to assist a witness, protect him, or provide him with food or other provisions.

Here, an ailing witness makes his way to Jerusalem on donkeyback. He is surrounded by escorts and armed companions.

New-Moon Witnesses Detained in Lod

The Talmud relates an interesting episode which took place one Sabbath in the city of Lod. Pairs of witnesses who had seen the new moon were on their way to the Great Court to give testimony. In Lod, however, they were detained by a man named Zefer, the mayor of Geder. He felt that because the court had certainly already received testimony from others, the continued journey of these witnesses was unnecessary, especially considering that it involved a desecration of the Sabbath.

The Sadducees and the Boethusians

The Talmud describes an attempt by the Boethusian sect to mislead the sages and thwart their calculation of the new moon. Two people were paid hefty sums of money to give false testimony of the new moon before the Great Court. One of the witnesses, however, secretly loyal to the sages, revealed the scheme to the judges. Here, the informer holds up the 200 silver coins he was given as bribery. The hirer (left) is about to receive his punishment—lashes.

The *Beit Ya'azek* Courtyard

In order to accommodate the new-moon witnesses, a special courtyard was constructed in Jerusalem called *"Beit Ya'azek."* In this courtyard, gathering witnesses were provided with a large meal. The sojourners were received in this warm manner so that they not hesitate to come in the future. In this painting, witnesses who have already given testimony mingle in the courtyard. At center, two arriving witnesses are being directed to the Chamber of the Great Court where they will give testimony.

Z.SMEKHOV

"The Day is Hallowed!" When the process of receiving witnesses was over, the head of the court would declare: "The day is hallowed!" and the people who had gathered before the Chamber of Hewn Stone would respond: "The day is hallowed! The day is hallowed!" At this point, the priests brought forth the *Rosh Hodesh* and Rosh Hashanah offerings, and the Levites began to perform their song for Rosh Hashanah.

Rabban Gamliel's Upper Chamber

This illustration portrays Rabban Gamliel's upper chamber in Yavneh where he and the Great Court received new-moon witnesses. On the wall are images of the moon's crescent in a variety of positions and sizes. Rabban Gamliel would make use of these pictures when questioning witnesses.

How the Torches Were Waved

This painting gives us a idea of the manner in which torches were wielded when sending word of the new moon to the Jews of the exile. A long cedar-wood pole was used so that the flame could be seen from afar. The man on the right is carrying a sack of flammable materials. The city of Pumbedita is discernible in the distance, "glowing like a huge bonfire" from its many torches proclaiming the new moon.

Torches Announce the New Moon

The proclamation of the new moon was signaled from mountaintop to mountaintop with large torches. The Mishnah provides a list of the names of the summits upon which these flares were lit, beginning in Jerusalem (in the center of the map) and reaching the Babylonian city of Pumbedita (upper right-hand corner). The Jews of Pumbedita would respond by climbing up on their rooftops and illuminating the city sky with torches.

Publicizing the advent of the New Moon without delay was necessary if the month's holidays were to be observed in their proper time.

Rabban Gamliel Receives Rabbi Yehoshua

The Mishnah relates a disagreement that arose between Rabban Gamliel and Rabbi Yehoshua over the criteria for accepting witnesses to sanctify the new moon. This discrepancy had practical implications regarding the dates of the High Holidays that year. Therefore, in order to prevent national discord, Rabban Gamliel ordered Rabbi Yehoshua to accept his decision, telling him: "Come to me with your staff and your money on the day that Yom Kippur falls according to your calculation." Here, Rabban Gamliel, head of the Sanhedrin, receives Rabbi Yehoshua with open arms as the latter submits to his order and publicly demonstrates acceptance of his ruling.

Messengers Are Sent Out

With the proclamation, "The day is hallowed!" by the Great Sanhedrin in the Chamber of Hewn Stone, messengers were sent out on horseback to publicize the sanctification of the month and to inform the Jews of the Diaspora as far away as Babylon and Persia regarding the accurate dates for upcoming Festivals and holidays.

Yom Kippur's Divine Heritage

The Day of Atonement's sacred service constituted a climax of all Temple ceremonies during the year. It was the only occasion on which the entire Divine service was performed by a solitary individual—the High Priest. On this day, sequence was essential. The Mishnah teaches us that if the High Priest reversed the order of even a single element of the Yom Kippur service, "he accomplished nothing." The High Priest's duties on the Day of Atonement were strenuous and complicated, and because each detail was so significant, the service is discussed at great length in both the Holy Scriptures (Lev. 16:1–34) and the Talmud (tractate *Yoma*).

The Talmud depicts the High Priest's presence in the Holy of Holies with vivid solemnity. When reading these texts, one momentarily forgets the earthly Temple in Jerusalem; one senses that the High Priest has entered God's own heavenly Temple and now stands before the Almighty Himself, seated on His exalted Throne of Mercy.

For example, Rabbi Yishmael ben Elisha recalled: "Once, when I entered the Holy of Holies to offer incense [on the Day of Atonement], I saw the Almighty God, the Lord of Hosts, sitting on a great and exalted throne. He said to me, 'Yishmael my son, bless me!'

"I said to Him, 'May it be Your will that Your kindness conquer Your anger, and Your trait of mercy rise above Your other traits so that You show compassion upon Your children and be lenient towards them,' and He nodded in agreement" (*Berakhot* 7a).

Elsewhere, we are told that when Rabbi Simeon the Just entered the Holy of Holies on Yom Kippur, he was accompanied by a mysterious figure: "In the year that Rabbi Simeon died, he informed his colleagues, saying, 'I will die this year.' When they asked him what made him so sure of this, he replied, 'Every Yom Kippur, an old man wearing white clothing and wrapped in a white shawl appears to me. He enters [the Holy of Holies] with me and exits with me. This year, however, an old man wearing black clothing and wrapped in a black shawl entered with me but did not exit with me.' After the Festival, Rabbi Simeon fell sick for seven days and then expired" (*Yoma* 39b).

It appears that the "old man" referred to here was the spirit of the patriarch Abraham. It must have been his duty to escort the High Priest in the Holy of Holies to help him secure atonement for the Jewish people on this fateful day.

On the Day of Atonement, the High Priest acted as emissary of the entire Jewish people. This fact is evidenced in the following source: "[On the eve of Yom Kippur,] the Elders of the High Court placed [the High Priest] in the custody of the Elders of the Priesthood who took him up to the Chamber of Avtinas.... [Before parting, the Elders of the High Court] said to him, 'Honorable High Priest, we are emissaries of the court and you are both our emissary and the emissary of the court; we adjure you by He Who rests His name in this house, not to change a single detail of everything that we have instructed you'" (*Yoma* 1:5).

This perhaps explains why it was necessary for Abraham's spirit to accompany the High Priest on this day. With the fate of the entire Nation of Israel resting on his shoulders, the High Priest had much to benefit from the father of the nation at his side.

Though much of the Temple service on Yom Kippur was carried out within the walls of the Sanctuary and behind the curtain of the Holy of Holies, the day's ceremony was never the exclusive possession or secretive rite of the High Priest or a group of priests. To the contrary, the details of this intricate service belong to the masses of Israel. They have been carefully analyzed in yeshiva study halls and affectionately intoned in synagogues for generations upon generations. Even young Jewish children learn to recite the Yom Kippur service and internalize its details—like the High Priest himself.

The High Priest Rehearses the Day of Atonement Services

In order to carry out his many duties on this fateful day, the High Priest begins to prepare himself a week in advance. He spends this period housed in a special chamber within the Temple, where he diligently reviews the laws pertaining to the service so that he will understand their practical application.

The Appointment of a Substitute for the High Priest

In the Temple's Palhedrin Chamber, a second priest is selected and prepared as a possible replacement for the High Priest—in the event that something unforeseen happens to disqualify him, rendering him unfit.

Nightlong Study in the Chamber of Avtinas

The night before Yom Kippur, some of the outstanding citizens of Jerusalem would refrain from sleeping and instead engage in Torah study all night long in the presence of the High Priest. They did this so that the latter would not be overtaken by sleep and would thus be able to attend to the Temple service in purity.

Familiarization with the Day's Offerings

On the morning of the eve of Yom Kippur, the High Priest was brought to the Gate of Nicanor which opened to the Women's Court. "Bulls, rams, and sheep," says the Mishnah, "would be led before him." This was done in order that he become familiar with the animals involved in the Day of Atonement service.

The High Priest's Oath

It is the eve of the Day of Atonement. The elders of the Sanhedrin take the High Priest up to the Chamber of Avtinas, where the incense for the Divine service is made. There, the elders administer a vow to the High Priest, in which the latter promises not to deviate from the instructions for attending to the incense service in the Holy of Holies.

The Immersion of the High Priest

The High Priest ascends a winding staircase to the ritual bath located above the Parvah Chamber. He presently wears the golden vestments, but when he emerges he will clothe himself in the white vestments. A white linen sheet would separate between the High Priest and onlookers. This was done in order to remind the people to purify themselves of sin on this day.

Immersion and Sanctification Before Changing Vestments

When the High Priest changed his vestments on the Day of Atonement he would first sanctify his hands and feet by pouring water upon them from a special gold vessel. Following this, he would remove his clothing and immerse. Emerging, the priest would put on the appropriate vestments and again sanctify his hands and feet. If the High Priest was old or delicate they would warm the water for him with hot iron balls.

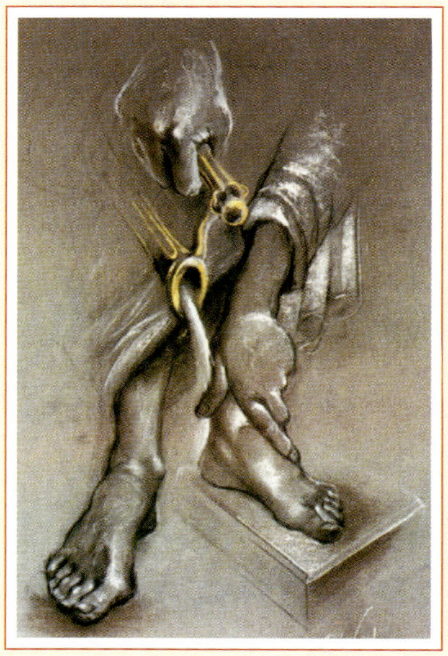

Sanctification from a Special Gold Vessel

On Yom Kippur, the High Priest would sanctify his hands and feet a total of ten times. Throughout the year, he would perform this ritual using the copper laver in the Courtyard like all the other priests. On this day, though, out of respect for the High Priest's status, a special gold vessel would be used. Here, we can see the unique manner in which the water was poured over the hands and feet.

The Daily Incense-offering on Yom Kippur

The incense service, representing the unity of Israel, is the most beloved service in God's eyes. The High Priest would offer incense three times on the Day of Atonement—twice upon the golden incense altar in the Sanctuary, as was done every day, and once in the Holy of Holies. Here, the High Priest faces north as he pours the incense on the golden altar, and a column of smoke rises up to the ceiling.

The Crowded Courtyard From the time the gates were opened at dawn, the Courtyard was filled with people. All eyes were turned to the High Priest, who, on that holiest day of the year,

would enter the most sacred place on earth—the Holy of Holies—to atone for Israel and to rectify the faults in their spiritual connection to their Father in Heaven.

The Day's Offerings

"You shall present a burnt offering for an appeasing fragrance to God: one young bull, one ram, and seven yearling sheep, making sure that all are devoid of blemish. . . . There shall also be one goat for a sin-offering . . ." (Num. 29:11).

The High Priest's Confession

Placing his hands on the head of the bullock, the High Priest would first confess his own sins and those of his household; later, he confessed over the bullock a second time, for his associate priests. While confessing, the High Priest utters the Divine name of God, at which point the priests and visitors in the Temple Courtyard kneel, prostrate themselves, and likewise confess.

Lots Drawn

The High Priest would place his two hands into the lottery box. In order to ensure that he could not possibly fix the outcome of the drawing, he was obligated to raise both lots from the box swiftly and simultaneously.

"Raise up your right hand!"

If the lot bearing the inscription "For God" is drawn with his right hand, the assistant declares, "My master, the High Priest! Raise up your right hand!"

Bringing the Two Goats

"And he shall take from the congregation of Israel two goats for a sin-offering . . . and he shall bring the two goats and present them before the Lord at the door of the Tent of Meeting. And Aaron shall cast lots upon the two goats: one lot for God; the other lot to Azazel" (Lev. 16:5–8).

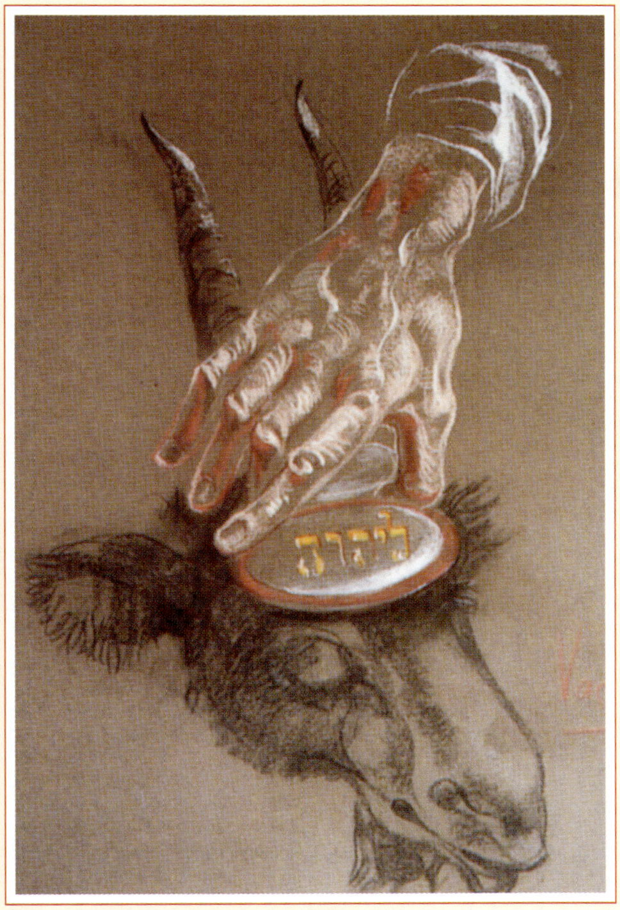

Placing the Lots on the Goats

If the lot for God came up in his right hand the High Priest would place it upon the head of the goat to his right; the lot for Azazel on the goat to his left. He would then proclaim, "A sin-offering for God."

Tying the Scarlet Skein

The High Priest would then tie a skein of scarlet wool around the horns of the goat that was to be sent away. The goat would then be brought to the Nicanor Gate, for it was through this gate that he would eventually depart.

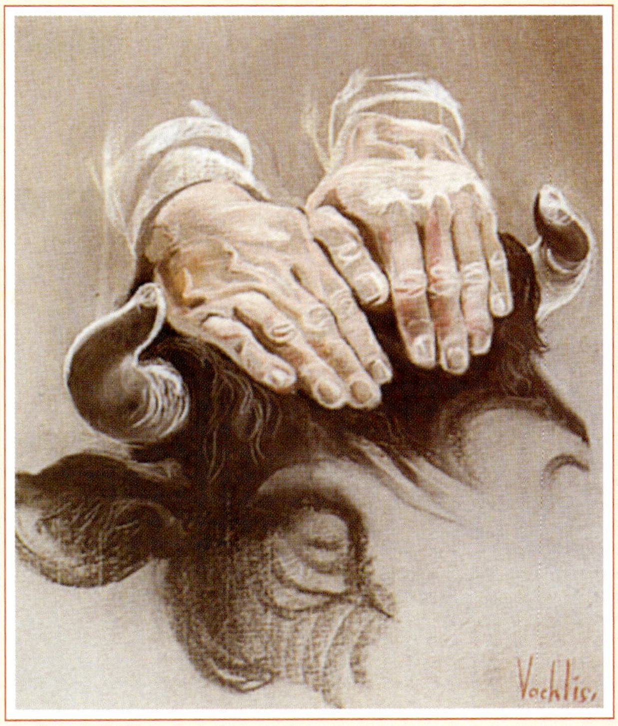

Laying of Hands on the Bull

In this manner would the High Priest place his two hands on the head of the bullock, "and make atonement for himself and his fellow priests" (Lev. 16:11).

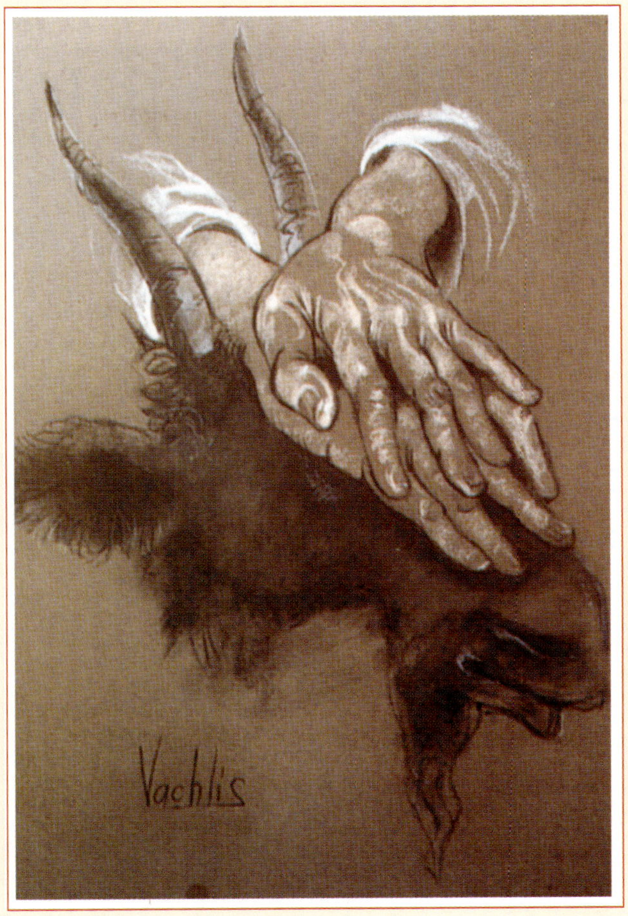

Laying of Hands on the Goat

The High Priest then "presses both his hands, the right one on top of the left, upon the live goat's head, and confesses on it all of Israel's sins, rebellious acts, and inadvertent misdeeds" (Lev. 16:21, *Targum Yonatan*).

The Fateful Lottery

Though the whole moving service of the Day of Atonement was marked by tense anticipation and deep feelings of repentance, surely one of the most dramatic moments of the day was the lottery which the High Priest conducted. The lottery process selected the scapegoat, which would be an atonement for Israel's sins. In this

portrayal, the Deputy High Priest stands to the High Priest's right, while the head of the family on duty stands to his left.

Confession Over the Scapegoat

"I beg of You, God!" the High Priest began his confession, "Your people, the House of Israel, has been iniquitous, sinned, and erred before you. O God, atone for the iniquities, sins, and errors . . . as it is written in the Torah of Moses Your servant, 'For on this day you shall be

atoned to purify you from all your sins, before God.'"

When the priests and the people in the Courtyard heard the Divine Name pronounced by the High Priest, they would kneel, prostrate themselves, and say, "Blessed be the Name of His glorious kingdom for all eternity."

The Slaughter of the Bull

Each and every movement of the High Priest's service on this day carried with it the power of spiritual renewal for all those present in the Holy Temple, based upon repentance and the desire for self-improvement. Here, having confessed upon the bullock, the High Priest himself slaughters it and receives its blood. He would then pass this vessel to his assistant who began mixing the blood so that it not congeal.

Bringing the Coals from the Altar

Now, seizing a gold fire pan, the High Priest climbs the altar and fills the pan with coals from the pile of wood on the altar's southwest corner. This pan of coals will later accompany the High Priest into the Holy of Holies.

Preparing to Enter the Holy of Holies

Next, the High Priest was brought a small shovel full of incense from the Avtinas Chamber. He would take a double handful of this fragrant mixture and pour it into a special gold vessel (on the small table). Having done this, the High Priest took the gold vessel in his left hand and the pan of coals in his right, and made his way to the Sanctuary.

Simple White Vestments

When entering the Holy of Holies on Yom Kippur, the High Priest would refrain from dawning his special gold garments and wear only simple white vestments. This was because gold recalled the Sin of the Golden Calf—and it was unseemly that the very symbol of Israel's guilt be worn at that moment wherein the nation sought complete vindication.

Into the Holy of Holies

The High Priest made his way through the Sanctuary, and walked between the curtains that divided between the Holy area and the Holy of Holies.

Offering Incense in the Holy of Holies

When the High Priest reached the Ark of the Covenant, he placed the pan between its two poles. He would then heap the incense on top of the coals, causing the entire room to fill with smoke. As we see here, the ark rested on the "Foundation Stone" which was three fingerbreadths high.

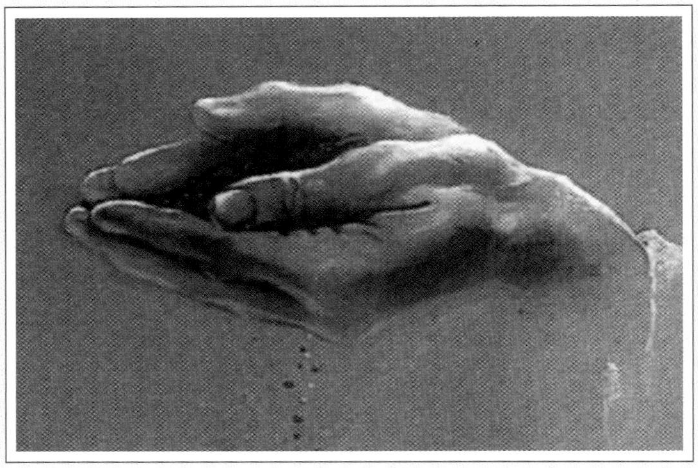

The First Handful of Incense

"He shall take a fire pan . . . along with a double handful of finely ground fragrant incense, and bring them into the [inner Sanctuary] beyond the cloth partition" (Lev. 16:12). The incense was made of eleven different spices that were combined in a unique mixture, the preparation of which, during the Second Temple era, was known only to the Avtinas family.

The Second Handful of Incense

Before heaping the incense on top of the coals, the High Priest was called upon to perform the most difficult task in his entire service: pouring the incense from the golden vessel into his own hands. In order to manage this, he had to clasp the vessel with his fingertips, or teeth, and, using his thumbs, edge the incense into his palms without spilling even the slightest amount.

Sprinkling the Blood Before the Ark

Having completed the incense service before the ark, the High Priest exits the Holy of Holies in order to fetch the blood of the bull which he previously slaughtered. He then returns and sprinkles it "with his forefinger, above the ark cover on the east side, and . . . seven times toward the ark cover" (Lev. 16:14).

Placing the Incense on the Foundation Stone

In the Second Temple era there was no longer an ark in the Holy of Holies. "There was," the Mishnah reports, "a stone which had been there since the days of the early prophets, called *'Shtiyah.'*" This stone was three fingerbreadths high, and it was here that the pan was placed.

A Short Prayer Before Exiting the Holy of Holies

The High Priest left the Holy of Holies walking backward, out of fear and humility. He then offered a short prayer in the outer chamber. The reason for not prolonging his prayer was so as not to cause the people to worry, for a High Priest who was unworthy or performed the service incorrectly might die in the Holy of Holies.

Sprinkling the Blood Before the Curtain

The Bible states, "He shall then carry out this same [procedure] inside the Communion Tent" (Lev. 16:16). This meant that the High Priest had to sprinkle both the blood of the bull and that of the goat, separately, toward the cloth partition—once in an upward direction and seven times downward. The blood was not sprinkled directly onto the cloth, but just before it so that it dripped upon the floor of the Sanctuary.

George

Once Upward, Seven Times Downward

The Bible tells us that on the Day of Atonement, the High Priest would sprinkle blood: once upward and seven times downward; first, before the ark and then before the cloth partition. These illustrations provide us with an understanding of what is meant by "upward" (left), and "downward" (right).

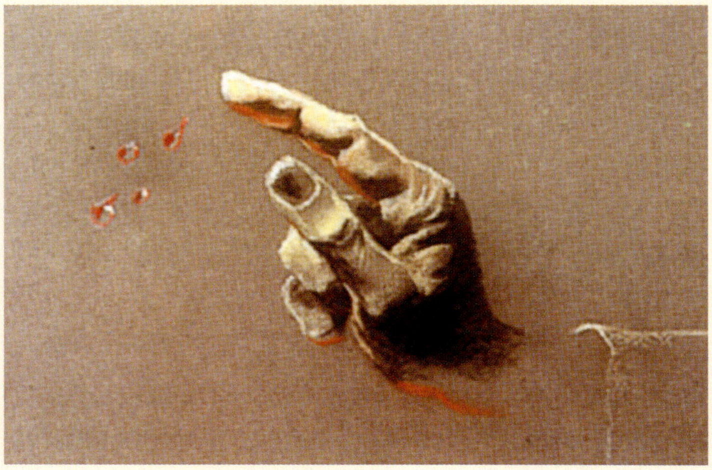

Sanctifying the Incense Altar

Next, the High Priest purifies and sanctifies the golden incense altar that is "before God." This was done by sprinkling a mixture of the bull's and the goat's blood on the four corners of the altar and then in the altar's center.

The Remaining Blood

Having completed the procedure of sprinkling blood in the inner and outer Sanctuaries, the High Priest would pour the remaining blood from its vessel onto the base of the southwest corner of the outer altar. There were two holes in the base—one to the south and one to the west. On the Day of Atonement, the blood was poured into the western hole.

Daughters of Jerusalem Dance in the Vineyards

Rabbi Shimon ben Gamliel reports that the Day of Atonement was one of the most joyous days of the year for the people of Israel. On this day, "the daughters of Jerusalem would go out in borrowed white attire . . . and dance circles in the vineyards."

Sending the Goat to the Wilderness

In this illustration, the High Priest is seen presenting the scapegoat to the one responsible for leading the animal into the Wilderness. The two stand under the Shushan Gate situated on the east side of the Temple Mount, for it was from here that the journey began. Visitors from near and far have come to be present for this special occasion, many of whom will even accompany the he-goat and its attendant for part of their journey.

"Take and Go!"

The Talmud informs us that the Jews of Alexandria had a custom of plucking the scapegoat's hair and saying, "Take and go!" By this they meant, "Take our sins and go to the Wilderness. Let our sins tarry here no longer." The priests, though, discouraged this practice and even constructed a special ramp in an attempt to put an end to it.

The Scapegoat on His Way

Ten huts were set up from Jerusalem to the cliff in the Wilderness, and at each one the man entrusted with escorting the scapegoat was offered food and drink; for, though he was obligated to fast on the Day of Repentance like everybody else, if his task became overbearing, he was permitted to eat. Nonetheless, tradition relates that not one of these messengers ever broke his fast.

Huts from Jerusalem to the Cliff in the Wilderness

This breathtaking representation provides us with a view of the route from Jerusalem to the Wilderness cliff where the scapegoat was destined to meet its end. Resting stations dot the way, and groups of anxious Jews are gathered at each stop, waiting to receive the goat and its attendant and to accompany them until the next station.

BARANOVSKY D 95

"A Serrated Land"

"The goat will thus carry all the sins away to a serrated land . . ." (Lev. 16:22). In keeping with this verse, the cliff over which the goat was thrown had to consist of sharp, jagged rocks. Here, the last of those parties which had accompanied the scapegoat to its final destination watches from a distance.

The Scapegoat on Top of the Cliff

Before pushing the goat backwards, the designated attendant would take part of the scarlet wool skein tied around the goat's horns and tie it to a rock. If, with the scapegoat's death below, this skein miraculously turned white, it was known that Israel's sins had been forgiven.

The Scapegoat's Fall

Rabbi Moshe Maimonides, the Rambam, writes that the scapegoat served as a source of atonement for all of Israel. With the animal's demise, he who had cast it from the cliff would exclaim, "May the transgressions of the Jewish people be likewise eradicated."

The Torah Reading in the Women's Court

Upon receiving word that the scapegoat had reached the Wilderness, the High Priest would read the portion describing the day's service (Lev. Ch. 16) from a Torah scroll. This reading was carried out on the steps leading from the Women's to the Priests' Courtyard, and, as we see in this illustration, many of those who participated would bring their own scrolls in order to follow along.

The Burning of the Bull and the Goat

"The bull and goat presented as sin-offerings, the blood of whom was brought into the Sanctuary to make atonement, shall be taken outside the camp" (Lev. 16:27). Here, a procession of eager onlookers accompanies the offerings out the northern gate of the city to a site known as "the Place of the Ashes." At center, a priest cautions the crowd, warning them not to mount the altar.

Disposing of the White Vestments

With the close of the day's service, the High Priest would dispose of his white vestments in a special compartment in the Temple. Here, assistants flank the High Priest in the Chamber of Pinchas, which served primarily as a storeroom for priestly garments. One holds the vestments worn by the High Priest in the morning; the other, those worn in the afternoon.

"He made a feast for his friends..."

Having emerged safely from the Holy of Holies, the High Priest would invite all those involved in preparing and successfully carrying out Yom Kippur service to join him in a celebrative feast. His face shone radiantly as he exited the Temple, and celebrants in the Courtyard escorted him home. The heads of the Sanhedrin (left) would also come to bestow their blessings upon the High Priest on this special occasion.

A Ram's Horn Blast Proclaims the Arrival of the Jubilee Year

In biblical times, a Jubilee year was proclaimed once every fifty years, and with its arrival all slaves were freed. In this illustration, a family of slaves bids farewell to its masters as word ar-

rives from the High Court in Jerusalem that the Jubilee year has commenced. Every Jew was obligated to blow from a ram's horn upon receiving this news.

The Proclamation of the Jubilee Year in the Sanhedrin

The Head of the Court gives the order to sound nine blasts on the ram's horn in proclamation of the Jubilee year's commencement. The biblical obligation to blow a ram's horn at the outset of the Jubilee year was fulfilled first by the Sanhedrin in the Temple's Chamber of Hewn Stone. From here, it spread throughout the land. To the right, now-free slaves receive the blasts joyously.

The Closing of the Gates

Just before sunset, the service of the day complete, Levite gatekeepers would push close the gates of the Sanctuary and the Courtyard. Whatever audience remained would make its way home at this point. According to the Jerusalem Talmud, the *"Neilah"* (closing) prayer recited today in the synagogue at the conclusion of the Day of Atonement services is an allusion to the closing of the Temple gates.

The Sukkot Festival: "Rejoice Before the Lord"

Of the three Pilgrim Festivals, Sukkot was celebrated with unparalleled joy.

Nowhere was this great wave of Sukkot joy felt so strongly as in the Temple. The multitudes would take their "four species" in hand and make their way to the Temple Courtyard to circle the altar and sing the festive *Hallel* prayer of thanks. In this manner, they would fulfill the commandment, "And you shall take for yourself a fruit of the citron tree, a palm frond, myrtle branches, and willows. You shall rejoice before the Lord your God for seven days..." (Lev. 23:40).

"Rejoicing before the Lord" during Sukkot was also expressed in song. More emphasis was placed on the musical performance of the Levitical choir at this time than during the rest of the year. Many of the converging pilgrims brought their own musical instruments and joined the Levitical ensemble in song. The sages teach that the Sukkot Festival was one of those rare occasions during the year when flutes were played in the Temple Court before the altar.

During the Sukkot Festival, the Holy City of Jerusalem took on an entirely new complexion. Streets, courtyards, roofs—wherever one looked, one saw makeshift thatch-roofed huts. Some of these "*sukkot*" belonged to the citizens of Jerusalem; others had been prepared for the many Festival pilgrims who flocked the city in great numbers.

Another spectacular Sukkot sight was the waves of people with their Festival species in hand. The Talmud testifies to this in the following account: "Such was the practice of the citizens of Jerusalem: when a person left his house, he did so with his four species in hand; when he went to the synagogue, he did so with his four species in hand; when he recited the *Shema* and prayed, he did so with his four species in hand; when reading from the Torah and reciting the Priestly Blessing, he placed the species on the ground; when he went to visit the sick or comfort mourners, he did so with his four species in hand; when he entered the study hall, he had his species cared for by his son, his servant, or an errand boy. From here we can see just how adamant they were when it came to fulfilling the commandments" (*Sukkah* 41b).

During Sukkot in the time of the Holy Temple, a unique offering with a special purpose was brought upon the altar. On each of the Festival's seven days, a descending number of bulls was brought as part of a burnt-offering. The total number of bulls offered was seventy (see Num. 29:12–34). The sages teach that these seventy bulls served as an atonement for the seventy primordial nations of the world (see Gen. 10). In other words, the offering of these sacrifices was intended to bestow a heavenly blessing upon all of the people of the world.

The precepts that needed to be fulfilled in the Holy Temple during the Sukkot Festival were so numerous and so time-consuming that there was practically no time to sleep. "Rabbi Yehoshua ben Hanina said: 'During the days of the Sukkot Water Libation Celebration, we barely got to sleep at all. The first hour of the day saw us attending to the daily sacrifice; following this, we were engaged in prayer; afterwards, the additional sacrifice; then, the additional prayer service; next, we went to the study hall; after studying, we ate and drank; after this, the afternoon prayer service; following this, the daily sacrifice of the afternoon; then, the Celebration of the Water Libation which lasted the entire night; and when that ended, we would start all over again!'" (*Sukkah* 53a).

The joy that permeated the city of Jerusalem during Sukkot was as colorful as it was manifold. It is our hope that through these illustrations the reader will receive a taste of the Sukkot Festival as it was in the days when the Holy Temple stood in the heart of the nation.

A Street in Jerusalem at Sukkot Time

As the citizens of Jerusalem prepare for the upcoming Sukkot Festival, the city's air is filled with excitement. Everyone is busy selecting the four species used for the holiday worship, and constructing "*sukkot*," temporary huts in which "every citizen in Israel" must dwell during the Festival.

Circling the Altar Each Day

"Every day," says the Mishnah, "they would circle the altar once and say, 'Please God, bring us salvation! Please God, bring us success!' . . . On the seventh day, they would circle the altar seven times" (*Sukkah* 4:5). In this illustration, the priests can be seen walking at the head of the procession which circles the altar, their four species in hand.

Gold Bands—Adornment of the Four Species

The commandment of the four species has always been greatly cherished by the Jewish people. In the time of the Temple, Jerusalem's wealthier citizens made a practice of adorning their species with gold bands as a show of adoration for this Divine precept. As is evident from this illustration, they would attach these bands to the upper area of the palm branch.

The Four Species in the Temple on the Sabbath

On Sukkot, many Jews chose to give their happiness full expression by going to the Temple to fulfill the commandment of waving the four species. Yet, because carrying objects from one domain to another is forbidden on Sabbath, it was necessary, when the first day of Sukkot fell on Sabbath, for citizens to bring their species to the Temple on Friday and leave them there overnight. Here, we see people bustling to find their species on Sabbath morning.

The Festival's Seventy Bulls

The total number of bulls offered in the Temple during the seven-day Festival of Sukkot was seventy. These seventy bulls represent the seventy primal nations of the world, and their offering was intended to bring heavenly blessing upon all of the nations. Here is an artistic portrayal of the *mussaf* offerings for the first day of the Festival.

A Holiday for the Whole World

The Talmud (*Sukkah* 55b) teaches that the seventy bulls offered in the Holy Temple served as atonement for the seventy nations of the world. Through the holiday's sacrificial requirements one senses that an inexorable bond links Sukkot with the Earth's peoples. The Creator Himself intended for Sukkot to be a holiday for the whole world.

Willow Branches from Motza

"There was a location below Jerusalem called Motza" (*Sukkah* 4:5). The sages tell us that court messengers would "go down there and pick willow branches and then return and place them alongside the altar." This was done on each of the days of the Sukkot Festival in fulfillment of the commandment to place willows alongside the Temple's altar. Here, we look on as the citizens of Motza and court messengers fell large willow trees and haul off their branches in the direction of the Temple.

Gold Basins for Willows on the Sabbath

In honor of the Sabbath, the priests in the Temple took care to prepare in advance willow branches for the public. These willow branches were placed in large gold basins, from which they were distributed by the priests to the congregants in the Courtyard.

Beating Willows on the Courtyard Floor

The Torah commandment to beat willows on the ground has great mystical meaning. Initially, it was performed only in the Temple. Later, however, the prophets Haggai, Zechariah, and Malachi introduced this custom on the last day of the Festival, even outside the Holy Temple.

A Flask Filled from the Spring of Siloam

During the celebration of the Festival of the Water Libation on Sukkot, the priests and Levites, accompanied by multitudes of people, descended to the Spring of Siloam each morning at dawn with great song and rejoicing. There, they filled a special golden flask with the sparkling spring water and brought it up to the Temple, where it was poured out on the altar.

Reaching the Water Gate The priest arrives bringing the water from the Siloam Spring to the Temple through the Gate of Water (right). "When the celebrants reached the Water Gate at the Holy Temple, rams' horns were sounded together with blasts from the silver trumpets" (*Sukkah* 4:9).

The Golden Water Libation Flask

This golden flask was designed for the Festival of the Water Libation. Water was drawn from the Siloam Spring and carried back to the Holy Temple in this vessel, where it was poured on the altar.

The Silver Water Libation Cup

In the Ceremony of the Water Libation, water is poured from a golden flask into a special silver cup which sits on the top of the altar. The water trickles through a small spout underneath the cup down to the bottom of the altar. This cup has been created by researchers and craftsmen at the Temple Institute.

The Wine and Water Libations in the Temple

On the southwest corner of the altar, two silver cups were fixed. Into these cups, wine and water libations were poured. The two cups were fashioned in such a way as to enable the wine and water to flow at the same pace, and reach the foundation of the altar simultaneously.

Trumpet Blasts Accompany the Willow Placement and the Libations

One of the more fabulous sights in the Temple. At the foot of the large outer altar, a tall willow bough is fixed in place so that the heads of its branches bend over the top of the altar; both water and wine libations are poured; and trumpets are sounded by priests from upon a marble table. This was a fitting grand finale to the nightlong festivity which accompanied the drawing of water from the Siloam Spring.

The Gold Water Libation Container

Because on the Sabbath it was impossible to bring water from the Siloam Spring, water was drawn and kept inside a large golden container on Friday. This container was placed in the Courtyard ready for the Sabbath water libation.

The Hollow at the Altar's Corner

The wine and water of the libations poured on the altar would flow through drainpipes and eventually reach a special hollow under the floor of the Courtyard. At the foot of the southwest corner of the altar, a large cavity was created through which it was possible to descend and clean out the residue which accumulated in this hole—as we see in this illustration.

A "Great Rectification"

Men, women, and children participated in the immense joy of the water libation—some directly, while others stood and watched. Because these festivities took place in the Women's Court, elevated balconies were constructed, enabling the women to watch the dancing of the wise men of the Sanhedrin from above. The sages referred to the introduction of these balconies, which prevented inadvertent levity, as a "great rectification."

Young Priests Light Up the Temple and Jerusalem

At the Celebration of the Water Libation, "great lamps of gold were erected, with four golden oil cups at the top of each. Four young priests-in-training would climb to the top, carrying immense oil cans with which they would fill the cups. Once lit, there was not a courtyard in Jerusalem that did not glow from the light of the celebration . . ." (*Sukkah* 5:3).

The Festival of the Water Libation

Sukkot was the time of the famed "Festival of the Water Libation," an occasion of such great joy and celebration that the sages of Israel declared, "Whoever has not seen the Festival of the Water Libation, has never experienced true joy." This celebration took place in the Women's Court. Here, as we see in this illustration, the learned and pious leaders of Israel would dance and sing before the Presence of God.

Men of Piety and Good Deeds Dance Before the Celebrants

The Mishnah relates that during the celebrations of the Water Libation Festival, the sages of the Sanhedrin danced joyfully before God, and juggled flaming torches. Rabban Gamliel juggled eight such torches, catching them one at a time without allowing them to touch one another. In this artist's rendition, a discerning eye can pick out the great sage in action.

"We turn our eyes to God"

On the steps leading up to the brass Nicanor Gates, while the Levites play musical instruments and the Israelites look on, the priest bearing the decanter for the water libation turns and faces the Sanctuary. The Mishnah (*Sukkah* 5:4) relates that during the procession down to the Siloam, when they reached the eastern gate, the people would turn and proclaim: "... As for us, we turn our eyes to God."

A Wooden Platform in the Courtyard

In preparation for the *Hak'hel* ceremony in the Temple, a large wooden platform was erected in the center of the Women's Court so that the congregants would be able to see the king reading from the Torah and hear his voice. In light of the words of Nehemiah the prophet, that "the people went forth . . . and made booths . . . in their courts, and in the courts of the House of God" (Neh. 8:16), it stands to reason that it was also necessary to build a *sukkah* for the king to read under. This painting gives us a sense of what preparations for the *Hak'hel* ceremony must have been like.

Gathering the People for the *Hak'hel* Ceremony

Regarding the *Hak'hel* ceremony, the Torah teaches, "You must gather together the people, the men, women, children, and proselytes from your settlements, and allow them to hear it" (Deut. 31:12). It was the priests who bore responsibility for carrying out this commandment, as is evident from this moving depiction. They would stand on street corners and in gateways, blowing on their trumpets and announcing the hour of the Torah-reading ceremony.

The *Hak'hel* Ceremony in the Women's Court

In the Women's Court of the Holy Temple, a temporary platform was erected where the King of Israel would read aloud from the Torah, as the entire congregation listened on. A special biblical commandment requires the king to gather the whole nation together for the *Hak'hel* ceremony once every seven years.

Youngsters Grab the Adults' Four Species

After the circling of the altar on the last day of Sukkot, Jewish children would teasingly snatch the adults' four species and eat their citrons. The adults, understanding that these games reflected the festive spirit of the day, would play along affectionately.

The *Shemini Atzeret* Additional Offering

On *Shemini Atzeret*, the eighth day after the beginning of the *Sukkot* Festival, a special *mussaf* (additional) offering was presented in the Temple. This time, though, the service involved only one ox. The sages have likened the offering of this single ox at Sukkot's conclusion to an intimate meal which God shares with His most beloved friend—Israel.

Smoke from the Altar After *Shemini Atzeret*

In Temple days, the direction of the smoke which rose from the altar at the departure of the *Shemini Atzeret* Festival served to indicate what sort of weather could be expected during the approaching winter. Here, the people look on anxiously, hoping to gain some insight regarding the coming year's harvest.

The Passover Festival: A Joy That Unites

While the entire Nation of Israel made the pilgrimage to the Holy Temple on each of the sacred Festivals, it would seem that the record for participants was set on Passover, with more people arriving in Jerusalem for that Festival than any other. One very basic reason for this is the simple fact that the Passover sacrifice is a holy obligation that by biblical law is incumbent upon both men and women alike. This differs from the other Festival offerings, which are only obligatory upon the men of the community. Furthermore, those who do not participate in the Passover offering face a most severe penalty: the biblical punishment of *karet* (literally, "to be cut off"), which is interpreted by some to mean premature or sudden death, and by others to be an indication of spiritual demotion in the future world. Clearly, all who had the ability made certain to be among those who arrived in Jerusalem for Passover.

The Talmud offers an example that can serve to illustrate the incredible numbers which converged upon Jerusalem for this holy occasion. It seems that one year, King Agrippa wanted to determine the exact number of the pilgrims who arrived to celebrate Passover, so he hit upon a unique idea for conducting a census. He instructed the High Priest who was officiating in the Temple: "Pay attention to the exact amount of offerings that are brought." And so the Priest set aside the offerings and numbered them . . . until the figure reached a staggering 1,200,000, which is twice the number of the Jews who participated in the Exodus from Egypt. And this figure does not include those who were impure and those who had not arrived in time! Because of these great numbers, the holiday was referred to as "Passover of density" (see *Pesachim* 64b).

It was the communal air of the Festival that made Passover unique; large numbers of pilgrims (sometimes as many as one hundred!) would band together, recline on couches and consume the meat of a single Pascal Lamb. Needless to say, such enormous gatherings instilled participants with feelings of unbounded joy and elevation.

Families brought more offerings to the Temple on this holiday than on any other. On the fourteenth of the month of Nissan, each family brought its Passover sacrifice, as well as a Festival peace-offering. These offerings were eaten together at the Passover *seder* meal with the *matzot* (unleavened bread) and *marror* (bitter herbs). The festive participants, united around the table, recounted the story of the Exodus from Egypt and praised God for the redemption from slavery.

As midnight approached, the participants of every household in Jerusalem ate their Passover sacrifices and went up to the roofs to sing the festive *Hallel* prayer of thanks before the Holy Temple. The overwhelming sense of joy and elation in Jerusalem knew no bounds; it permeated every street, every courtyard, every house. An unparalleled feeling of belonging and brotherhood encompassed all the participants, and their great sentiment of freedom and redemption was the unsurpassed height of true religious experience. Indeed, a popular expression in the Talmud coined by the rabbis recalls that the very walls of Jerusalem shook and "the roofs were shattered" from the sounds of this joy.

It is our hope that the following illustrations and their accompanying explanations succeed in conveying something of Passover's special content and elating spirit.

These impressive representations, which depict the various aspects of the Passover Festival as once observed in Jerusalem and the Temple, are especially valuable because they educate us regarding many of the holiday's unique laws. Collectively, these sacred laws impressed upon Festival pilgrims a sense of joy and sanctity, feelings which were the cherished and exclusive possession of all who merited entering the gates of the Holy City.

Pilgrim Routes to Jerusalem—and the "Land of the Cutheans"

Ritually pure pilgrims who wished to reach Jerusalem without becoming defiled would follow certain routes that were presumed to be uncontaminated. Such routes existed on the coastal plain and in the Jordan Valley. The hills of Samaria, though, known as the "Land of the Cutheans," were deemed ritually impure; only the ritually impure could follow this route.

Court Messengers Proclaim, "Come, let us go up to Jerusalem!"

Festival pilgrims on their way to Jerusalem would spend their nights in certain designated cities which were scattered throughout the country. Caravans arrived at these centers from all over, and the numerous travelers would sleep in the open air of the city streets. Waking up in the morning, the overseer would cry out, "Arise, and let us go to Zion, to the house of the Lord our God."

Road Repairs for Festival Pilgrims

A month before the arrival of Passover, laborers were sent out to restore weather-beaten roads in anticipation of the many throngs of Festival pilgrims. A special Temple official was appointed to oversee this important task which also involved digging and repairing wells for drinking water, and seeing to the many ritual baths, without which entrance into the Holy Temple would be impossible.

Sabbath Observance in the Outdoors

The pilgrimage to Jerusalem for the Festival often involved Sabbath observance in open fields. Keeping the Sabbath under such conditions was not always simple. The laws connected to transferring objects from various domains on Sabbath made matters particularly tricky. In order to make the plight of these sojourners easier, the rabbis instituted measures which effectively allowed for watering the animals from wells in the field, an ordeal which would otherwise have been nearly impossible.

Modiin: A Central Way-station on the Road to Jerusalem

Traffic on the road to Jerusalem. Pilgrims from the Coastal Plain passed through the city of Modiin and then continued past Beth-horon on their way to the Holy City. Because of its proximity to Jerusalem, Modiin served as an important crossroad for the multitude of Temple-

bound travelers. The Talmud states that sometimes the congestion caused by "traffic jams" of caravans and convoys in such places was so great that the road swelled with travelers who were unable to continue their journey due to the sheer number of people present.

It was here, in Modiin, that the first stirrings of the Maccabean rebellion began, when Mattathias inspired his five sons and other followers to attack Greek soldiers and officials who had come to collect taxes and force the people to worship the Greek gods.

Festival Pilgrims Purify the Way to Jerusalem

A number of weeks before the arrival of the holiday, court messengers were sent out to check the road. It was their job to mark with whitewash any graves that they discovered in the vicinity of the roads (left) in order that the ritually pure not unsuspect-

ingly become contaminated on the way to the Temple.
Occasionally, pilgrims happened upon a field containing a grave which was accidentally ploughed over and the bones of which may have been strewn throughout. The sages devised ways of entering such fields without contracting ritual impurity (right).

Temple Bound

"Three times a year, all your males will appear before the Presence of the Lord..." (Ex. 23:17). Pilgrims excitedly approach their long-awaited destination: the Temple Mount. All people, regardless of their spiritual level, would come to Jerusalem to uplift their spiritual energies. They would enjoy the fulfilling experience and sense of holiness only possible in such a close encounter with the Divine.

Priestly Children

According to biblical law, those who prepare the mixture of the water and heifer's ashes must themselves be pure. However, since the impurity caused by exposure to death is so common, it was a challenge to find someone pure! During the Temple era, a special method was devised to circumvent this difficulty. The children of priestly families were raised from birth in special courtyards where no impurity could penetrate, because they were surrounded by stone on all sides. When the children were old enough, they rode down to the Siloam Spring on oxen. Boards were placed across these animals as an added precaution that no impurity from the ground should affect the young riders. There, at the pure waters of Siloam, the children would draw the water and bring it back to the Holy Temple.

Preparing the Purifying Waters

A priest pours water, which was brought from the Siloam Spring in a stone vessel, into a stone container, and a small amount of ashes from the red heifer is added.

The Burning of the Red Heifer

Of all the unique methods used to institute purity in the Temple, one of the most significant and important is the process of purification through the ashes of the red heifer. The heifer was brought to the Mount of Olives, the Mountain of Anointment, on a special bridge connecting it to the Temple Mount. A large assembly, including the Elders of Israel, attended. A huge pile of wood awaited the heifer. As the animal is consumed by fire, the priest added cedar and hyssop wood which were tied together by a band dyed with scarlet obtained from the "*shani*" snail.

Pounding the Ashes of the Red Heifer

After the burning of the red heifer, its ashes were crushed with long clubs by the priests. Upon completing this process, the ashes were sifted so that a powder was obtained.

Purity Maintenance for Festival Pilgrims

Pilgrims arrive in Jerusalem. As the Festival approached, special measures were taken to safeguard ritual purity in the Holy City. The streets were swept clean daily. Those who were ritually pure walked down the middle of the road; those who were ritually impure kept to the sides. Here, vendors are seen selling animals for Festival offerings while prospective buyers check for disqualifying blemishes.

Sprinkling the Purifying Waters

Priests sprinkle water mixed with the heifer's ashes upon a family that contracted ritual impurity. This procedure took place on the third and seventh day after defilement. The family members stand before the priest, clothed in their impure garments and holding impure vessels. According to Jewish law, a few drops is enough to render one ritually pure.

Preparing Ritually Pure Earthenware Utensils

An earthenware vessel that has become defiled cannot regain ritual purity unless it is first broken. Hence, potters were especially careful when it came to protecting the purity of their wares for the Festival pilgrims. The sages ruled that because the inhabitants of Modiin were priests who knew how to maintain purity, all earthenware vessels manufactured in that city were considered pure.

The Ritual Baths of Jerusalem The ritual baths in Jerusalem were unique in that tainted incoming vessels were brought through one entrance while ritually pure vessels were taken out via a separate route. This depiction serves to illustrate the procedure: impure utensils are brought through the lower entrance to the right, while pure vessels are carried out the exit at the top of the stairs.

The Half-shekel

In the Temple era, all male Jews were annually required to bring a half-shekel contribution to the Temple for the purpose of buying communal sacrifices. From the beginning of the Hebrew month of Adar, notice was served to the public to prepare their half-shekel contributions. Festival pilgrims would bring contributions from cities and towns in the Land of Israel and abroad to the Temple treasurers.

The Festival Offerings

On each of the seven days of Passover, two bulls, one ram, seven lambs, and a goat were offered up in the Temple. On the day following the first day of Passover, a single male sheep was brought as a burnt-offering together with the yearly *Omer* barley offering (left).

The Family and Holiday Offerings

It is forbidden, on the three Pilgrim Festivals, to come to the Temple "empty handed" (Deut. 16:16–17). Here, a family makes the journey to Jerusalem for the Passover Festival with all of the necessary offerings.

The Chamber of the Half-shekel

The half-shekel contributions as well as other more direct donations were kept in a special room in the Temple called the Chamber of the Half-shekel. Three times a year, Temple treasurers would fill sacks of coins from this chamber in order to purchase animals for communal offerings. It was forbidden for the one who entered this chamber to wear any kind of apparel that might cause him to be suspected of having pocketed donation money.

Preparing to Enter the Temple Mount

One who intends to enter the Temple Mount must be prepared to observe the biblical commandment to behave with the utmost respect towards the Sanctuary. This means, among other things, removing one's shoes before entering. In this illustration, father and son prepare to enter the Temple through the Hulda Gate with their Passover offering.

Receiving the Festival Pilgrims

All of the assistant priests and Levites and Temple officials went out to greet the arriving Festival pilgrims, and all of the tradesmen of Jerusalem left their work to stand and greet them as they entered the gates of the city: "Our brothers from such and such a place, welcome, and peace unto you!"

Two Thanks-offering Loaves Announce the Prohibition of Leaven

The Mishnah teaches us that on the morning of Passover Eve, two thanks-offering loaves were placed out in the open on a certain balcony of the Temple Mount. So long as the loaves rested there, the people knew that it was still permissible to eat leavened foods. When one loaf was removed, the consumption of leaven became forbidden; the removal of the second loaf indicated that it was time to burn all remaining leaven.

Festival Hospitality Customs in Jerusalem

Hospitality was one of the traits which characterized Jerusalemites in Temple times. Such hospitality found fullest expression during the Pilgrim Festivals. On such occasions, "there was a great custom in Jerusalem; locals would spread a towel over the entrance. So long as the towel was spread there, guests would enter; when the towel was removed, there was no longer consent to enter" (*Tosefta, Berakhot* 4:8).

Z SMEKHOV

Festival Pilgrims Enter the Temple Courtyard

The ceremony of bringing the Passover offering was one of the most important events in the Holy Temple. The Talmud contains many accounts of both the pilgrimage and the sacrificial ceremony in Second Temple days. These descriptions include the sight of the huge Temple gates opening, and the vast multitudes of joyous people streaming into the beautiful and majestic Holy Temple Courtyard. Trumpet blasts were sounded and the Levitical choir sang.

Passover Eve in the Temple Courtyard

Jewish law forbids many forms of carrying on the Sabbath. Therefore, when the fourteenth of Nisan, the day on which the Passover lamb must be offered, was a Sabbath, pilgrims would remain in the Temple until the day's departure. Then, each celebrant would take his lamb to wherever he was staying in Jerusalem.

Offering the Passover Sacrifices

The priests, clad in white, stood in long lines before the altar; in one line they held silver vessels, and in the other line, vessels of gold. With these vessels they received the blood of the sacrifice and sent the vessel up the line to the priest standing closest to the altar, who dashed the blood against the foundation of the altar.

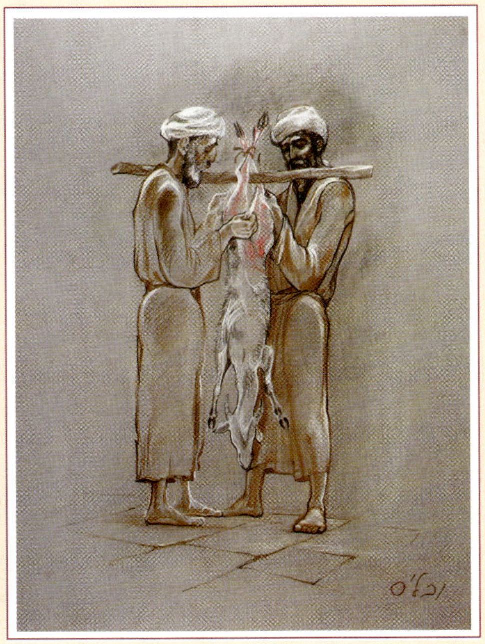

Preparing the Passover Sacrifice

There were special iron hooks attached to walls and to pillars in the Temple Courtyard. Here, the lamb's slaughterer would skin his animal and cleanse the carcass in preparation for the offering of its parts and for its eventual roasting.

Three Groups of Festival Pilgrims Slaughter the Pascal Lamb in the Courtyard

"When the first group entered and the Courtyard was full, the gates were closed after them. The Levitical choir stood by on their platform and sounded blasts from the *shofar* ram's horn, and silver trumpets. . . . When their service is concluded, the first group exits the Courtyard and is followed by the next group, and so on" (*Pesachim* 64).

The Courtyard Altar

A grandfather shows his grandson the priests performing the Festival service on the altar. Portions of the Passover offering were placed in a tray and taken up the ramp of the altar to be consumed thereupon.

Exiting the Temple with the Passover Sacrifice

When the first group of pilgrims finished slaughtering their lambs, they left the Courtyard carrying their lambs on their backs. The second and third groups entered, in turn, attended to their offerings, and left the Temple on their way to roast the Passover sacrifice whole, in keeping with the biblical requirement.

The Levitical Choir on Passover and Other Festivals

Within the Court of Israel, just inside the copper Nikanor Gates, the Levitical choir sang while standing upon a special platform that faced the outer altar. This grand ensemble consisted of vocalists (left) and musicians (right) who performed daily during the morning and evening wine libations. Their stage comprised three levels, and they played on four types of musical instruments: trumpets (top row), harps (bottom row, left), lyres (bottom row, center), and cymbals, which were used by the conductor of the ensemble.

This illustration captures the Levitical choir as it accompanies the Passover Sacrifice and leads the festive *Hallel* prayer of thanks. On Festivals and other special occasions, scores of vocalists and musicians from throughout the land would join the Levites in song. At such times even flautists (middle row, left, in blue robes) joined the ensemble.

Z.SMEKHOV

Rinsing Down the Temple Courtyard

When members of the public finished presenting their Passover offerings, the Temple Courtyard had to be thoroughly washed down. To this end, the entire area was flooded with water. Priests who continued in their Divine service were careful to walk on elevated walkways so as not to dirty their vestments.

"Mah Nishtanah" As the *seder* participants look on, the son poses the "four questions" to his father. In the course of the evening, they spoke of the miracles of the Exodus, ate *matzah* and bitter herbs dipped in *charoset*. At right, attendants enter carrying the roasted Passover sacrifice.

Roasting the Passover Lamb

With all of Israel in their multitudes converging at once to bring their Passover offering to the Holy Temple, special accommodations had to be made which would insure order. Ovens for roasting the Passover sacrifices were set up throughout the city, for after the sacrifice is offered, it will be taken by each family and group, and roasted in a special manner as prescribed by law, to be eaten in the evening at the *seder*.

Recounting the Exodus from Egypt

The festive *seder* participants, united around the table, recount the story of the Exodus from Egypt and praised God for the redemption from slavery—and for bringing them to the hallowed courts of the Temple where they could worship Him together in Jerusalem as free men.

Groups Gather for the Passover *Seder*

An illustration depicting how the Passover *seder* was conducted on the first night of Passover in Temple times. Several groups conduct their *seder* at once, and the tables are laden

with the Passover sacrifice, the *matzah* (unleavened bread), and wine. Those present recline on their left side (as required by Jewish law) on couches that were typical during the Roman era.

Merchants Open Wine Jugs for Festival Pilgrims

When it came to ritual purity, the sages gave special consideration to the city of Jerusalem during the Pilgrim Festivals. Throughout the year, if a jug of wine stood open within reaching distance of the public it could no longer be considered ritually pure. During the Festivals, though, because the populace as a whole was careful about ritual purity, such wine maintained its uncontaminated status.

Bakers Begin Kneading Dough for Festival Pilgrims

Not unlike wine, the rule concerning bread during the Festival was that it remain ritually pure even in places where it was handled by the public. This, as noted, was due to the fact that the masses were stringent when it came to maintaining ritual purity during the Festivals. With the holiday's departure, such bread was once again considered impure.

Songs of Praise on the Rooftops of Jerusalem

As midnight approached, the participants of every household in Jerusalem went up to the roofs for the singing of the festive *Hallel* prayer of thanks. All were affected by this special atmosphere as the sound of the beautiful prayers burst forth from every house. As the joyous sound of song echoed off the mountains surrounding Jerusalem, so too the Joy of the Festival of Freedom and Redemption surrounded the Jewish people.

The Barley Harvest

On the 16th day of Nissan, the barley to be used for the *Omer* offering was harvested in a grand public event. All of the inhabitants of the surrounding villages would gather together, and the barley would be cut in a great ceremony. This procedure emphasized the inaccuracy of the Boethusians' interpretation of the Bible. The Boethusians, a sect which did not believe in the Oral Tradition, taught that the barley could be harvested only on a Saturday night.

Omer Sieving in the Temple Courtyard

After harvesting the *Omer*, the priests would bring the barley in boxes and baskets to the Temple. There, on the eastern side of the Courtyard, the newly ripe grain was beaten, roasted, and sifted in thirteen sieves. A handful of the resulting flour was burned on the altar, and the rest was eaten by the priests.

Adding Olive Oil and Frankincense to the *Omer* Offering

The Bible states that the first grain offering must consist of fresh barley kernels roasted in a perforated pan, and then ground into a coarse meal. "You must," the verse continues, "place olive oil and frankincense on it . . ." (Lev. 2:15). This illustration provides us with an idea of how the once-yearly commandment was carried out.

The *Abuv*

An apparatus containing a perforated pan above and a receptacle for hot coals below. It was used for roasting the newly ripe barley for the *Omer* offering.

Waving the *Omer* Offering

Next, the priest must "wave the *Omer* before God" (Lev. 23:11). This act was carried out in front of the northeast corner of the altar while the priest stood facing the west.

Offering Handfuls from the *Omer*

The final step in the presentation of the *Omer* offering involved scooping out a handful of flour from the meal mixture and placing it in the fire on the altar. This completed, a single male sheep was brought as a burnt-offering. From this point on, grain from the new harvest could be eaten.

Breaking Earthenware Bowls from Which Sin-offerings Were Eaten

According to biblical law, an earthenware vessel from which the meat of a sin-offering was eaten must be broken, as the verse states, "Any earthen pot in which it is cooked must be broken" (Lev. 6:21). Indeed, some authorities maintain that earthenware vessels must be destroyed regardless of what type of offering was consumed therein. Here, priests shatter vessels from which they have just finished eating sin-offerings.

Presenting the *Omer* at the Foot of the Altar

After waving the *Omer* at the northeast corner of the altar, the priest presents this first grain offering before the southwest corner of the altar. This procedure was required for nearly all meal-offerings.

Gold Plaques from the Sanctuary are Displayed Before the Public

"The entire Sanctuary was overlaid with golden plaques. Each of these tablets was a square cubit in diameter and the size of a *dinar* (a common small coin) in width. In honor of the Pilgrim Festivals they were removed from the walls of the Sanctuary and put out for display upon the stairway leading to the Temple Mount. This was done so that Festival pilgrims could "observe the beauty and perfection of their (the artisans') work" (*Pesachim* 57a).

New Grain for Sale in the Jerusalem Marketplaces

Upon completion of the *Omer* offering in the Courtyard, pilgrims leaving the Temple would find the marketplaces of Jerusalem already overflowing with grain products from the new harvest. The Mishnah informs us that the practice of harvesting the new grain before its time was frowned upon by the sages.

Repaying the Hospitality of Jerusalemites

Jewish law forbade receiving payment from Festival pilgrims for accommodations provided during the holiday. As a result, before leaving, pilgrims would customarily present their hosts with whatever remained of their Festival goods. Here, a family of pilgrims has presented its hosts with the skin of a goat which was brought as an offering and a jug that they had used for keeping wine.

Displaying the Showbread Table and Menorah Before Festival Pilgrims

During Festivals, there was a custom to display the Temple's sacred vessels before Festival pilgrims. The Jerusalem Talmud relates that the pilgrims would be shown the ninety-three sacred vessels which were used in the Temple service. In this illustration, priests lift up the table and menorah for all to behold. At the same time, celebrants are asked to keep their distance in order to maintain the ritual purity of these sacred objects.

The Shavuot Festival: "These Are the Firstfruits"

The word *Shavuot* literally means "weeks"; Shavuot is thus known as the Festival of Weeks. It is so called because it culminates the seven-week period of counting which begins on the second day of Passover, when the *Omer* barley offering is brought to the Temple. Shavuot is also known as the Festival of the Giving of the Torah because it is the anniversary of the Revelation of the Law at Mount Sinai.

In the Bible, Shavuot is called the "Day of the Firstfruits" and the "Feast of the Harvest." Indeed, when the Temple stood, it was the agricultural aspect of this day which received fullest attention. At that time, the central feature of Shavuot was the bringing of the "twin loaves" offering in the Temple. This offering consisted of two large loaves baked from the newly harvested wheat crop.

There was a different type of offering, though, which each Jew brought from the firstfruits of his own soil to the priest in the Temple Courtyard. This offering came from the seven kinds of fruit with which the Land of Israel is specially favored. At Shavuot, however, the majority of these fruits had not yet ripened. Only wheat and barley had reached a state where they could be harvested and brought to the Temple; the other five fruits—figs, grapes, pomegranates, dates, and olives—did not see maturity until later in the course of the summer.

The Mishnah teaches: "When a person goes down to his field and sees (for the first time) a ripe fig or a ripe cluster of grapes or a ripe pomegranate, he binds a reed-grass ribbon around it and says, 'These are the firstfruits'" (*Bikkurim* 3:1). The three fruits mentioned here, though, do not ripen until the middle of the summer, well after Shavuot.

When, then, were the majority of the firstfruits brought to the Temple? It would appear that they were brought on the fifteenth of the month of *Av*. At this time of the year the three fruits mentioned above reached maturity. Unlike figs, grapes and pomegranates, dates and olives do not ripen until later, at the end of the summer.

The Mishnah (*Taanit* 28a) describes how once, in the days of the Second Temple, the Roman Empire enacted a decree which outlawed the bringing of firstfruits to Jerusalem. In order to enforce this law, roadblocks were set up on the routes leading to the Holy City. Yet, many faithful Jews refused to be beaten. What did they do? They prepared baskets of firstfruits, covered them over with figs, and set out for Jerusalem on the Fifteenth of *Av*. When they reached the roadblocks they were questioned regarding their destination. "We are on our way to the public mortar up ahead," they responded. "We have brought our pestles with us in order to make fig cakes from our figs." Once past the guards, the pilgrims uncovered their fruits, decorated them in their baskets and brought them up to Jerusalem.

From the foregoing account it becomes evident that while Jews indeed began bringing their firstfruits to the Temple on Shavuot, the principal date for this ceremony arrived some ten weeks later, on the Fifteenth of *Av*. This was a unique pilgrimage, quite independent of Shavuot, dedicated to the expression of heartfelt thanks for God's bounty and the presentation of the beginning of one's harvest to Him.

The illustrations which follow allow us to learn more about these and other issues bound up with the Shavuot Festival. May it be God's will that these depictions speedily become a tangible reality, precipitating the fulfillment of the words of our age-old supplication, "Allow our eyes to see Your compassionate return to Zion."

Firstfruits

"When a person goes down to his field and sees (for the first time) a ripe fig or a ripe cluster of grapes or a ripe pomegranate, he binds a reed-grass ribbon around it and says, 'These are the firstfruits . . .'" (*Bikkurim* 3:1).

Shavuot — Festival of the Firstfruits

Shavuot approaching, a family prepares for the pilgrimage by gathering the fruits that have been specially marked with a weed-grass ribbon. These are literally the "first" fruits that have ripened, and will therefore be brought to the Holy Temple. In addition to this produce, a goat and some doves are being readied. They too will be presented as offerings in Jerusalem.

Pilgrims on the Road

An illustration depicting caravans of pilgrims making their way along the road that will lead them to Jerusalem and the culmination of their journey, the Holy Temple. There

they will present the priests with their firstfruit offerings, which they carry along with them, and they will offer the holiday sacrifices—the ox and the sheep—which accompany the festive procession.

The Gathering Before the Pilgrimage

"The populace that lives in the vicinity of the Assembly Head (who is responsible for the priests and Levites, and also for the pilgrimage to Jerusalem) gathers together in his home town, and everyone sleeps the night in the town's streets.

They do not enter into the houses, to circumvent becoming exposed to ritual impurity (which would disqualify them from making the pilgrimage to the Temple). Waking up in the morning, the overseer would cry out, 'Arise, and let us go to Zion, to the house of the Lord our God'" (*Bikkurim* 3:2).

BARANOVSKY D
96

Firstfruit Baskets

An ox with gold-plated horns is led before a group of pilgrims as they approach Jerusalem (above), while firstfruits are carried in baskets on their owners' heads (right). There was a custom that pilgrims who were late in coming would decorate the horns of their animal offerings with silver rather than gold.

Approaching the Holy City

Countless streams of pilgrims made their way to Jerusalem from towns and villages all over the land, in large groups and individually. As the caravans of pilgrims drew near to Jerusalem and the Holy Temple, an ox with gold-plated horns was led before them, and flutes were played as the procession advanced. As they made their way, they sang out, "I was happy when they said to me, let us go to the House of the Lord" (Ps. 122:1; Jerusalem Talmud, *Bikkurim* 3:5).

Bringing the Firstfruits

Children, each one carrying a separate basket, accompany their father in the bringing of the firstfruits to the Temple. By bringing all of his children with him, this father is upholding the letter of the biblical verse which commands: "Let each of your males be seen . . ." (Deut. 16:16).

The Seven Favored Fruits

The choicest manner of fulfilling the commandment to bring the firstfruits to the Temple was by arranging each type of fruit in a separate basket—one basket for each of the seven kinds of fruit with which the Land of Israel is specially favored. The baskets were arranged one on top of the other, in ascending order of importance; hence, the bottommost basket contained barley. It was followed by wheat, olives, dates, pomegranates, and figs.

King Agrippa Brings the Firstfruits to the Temple

As Festival pilgrims bring their firstfruit offerings to Jerusalem in accordance with the biblical commandment, King Agrippa enters into the Holy Temple carrying a golden basket of fruit. The fruits were carried in baskets upon the shoulder, and even the King of Israel conducted himself in the same manner as the simple folk.

Festival Pilgrims Arrive in Jerusalem

"And you shall rejoice for all the goodness which the Lord your God has given to you and your household" (Deut. 26:15). Festive pilgrims arrive in Jerusalem, dressed in their holiday finery, singing joyously and playing musical instruments.

Khvedantsevich Dmitry

Presenting the Firstfruits in the Courtyard

The experience of bringing the firstfruits to the Temple served to unite the entire nation. By expressing heartfelt thanks for God's bounty and presenting the beginning of one's harvest to Him, a circle was closed as nature's produce was returned to its origin. The ceremony was spiritually elevating, and everyone felt deep reverence, awe, and joy as they realized that it is the Holy One alone who is the source of all blessing. Here, we see pilgrims in the Courtyard of the Temple performing the various steps of the firstfruit offering ceremony.

The Declaration of the Firstfruits

The owner of the firstfruits stands before the priest holding the basket on his shoulder. The priest would lead the pilgrim in reciting the biblical verses beginning with, "An Aramean destroyed my father" (Deut. 26:5).

The Waving of the Firstfruits

The priest then receives the basket from its owner and waves it in the prescribed manner.

Placing the Basket "Before God"

After completing the recitation of the biblical verses, the owner would set down his basket of firstfruits in the Courtyard, in accordance with the verse, "And you shall place it before the Lord, your God" (Deut. 26:11).

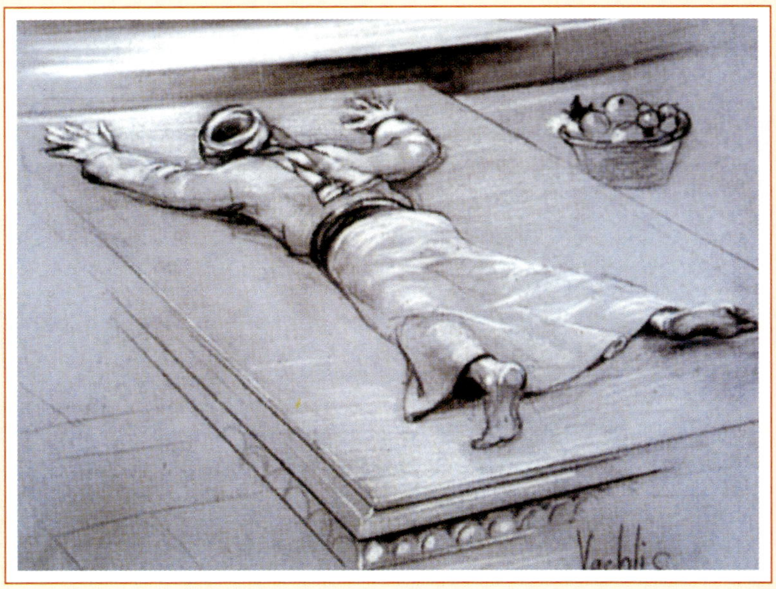

Prostration Before God

The final stage in the bringing of the firstfruits to the Holy Temple involved bowing down before God. Having performed this act, the pilgrim would rise and exit the Courtyard.

The Shavuot Offerings

On Shavuot, a total of twenty-six animal offerings were presented in the Temple. Two lambs were brought as peace-offerings (closest to us in this illustration) which accompanied the Festival's two communal-offering loaves of leavened bread. In addition, there were the fixed Festival offerings (the next group of animals in the distance) and additional offerings (the herd following them), together with the regular daily burnt offerings (at the head of the procession).

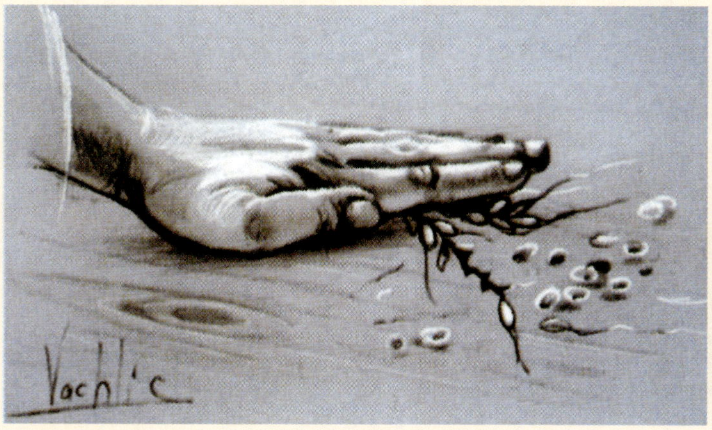

"Rubbing and Beating" for the Twin Loaves Offering

Once a year, on the Shavuot Festival, two loaves of leavened bread were brought as a communal offering in the Temple. Preparing the wheat kernels for this special "twin loaves" offering called for a unique procedure. Instead of resorting to the standard practice of threshing and winnowing, a method of "rubbing and beating" was employed to remove the seeds from the fiber and chaff.

Flour Preparation for the Twin Loaves Offering

After the rolling and pounding procedure was completed, the kernels of wheat were ground into a very fine flour. This flour was, in turn, sifted and sieved twelve times, so that what finally resulted were two tenths *ephah* of exceedingly pure, high-quality flour — one tenth for each of the two loaves.

The Kneading and Baking of the Twin Loaves

Each of the two loaves was kneaded and baked separately. They were rectangular in shape, seven handbreadths long and four handbreadths wide, and, according to some authorities, the loaves were molded such that there be hornlike protrusions on each of their four corners. When removed from the oven, the bread was placed onto another tray, so that it not be ruined.

Trumpets and Flutes Are Played at the Bringing of the Twin Loaves

As the Levitical choir performs (right) and the wine libation is poured (far left, on the altar), the special twin loaves bread offering is presented together with lambs for peace-offerings. Through this unique offering the people of Israel expressed their thanks to God for the world's heavenly blessing: nature's growth. So too, each individual shows his appreciation for his own sustenance, and that which God abundantly provides for all life on earth.

The Waving of the Twin Loaves and the Sheep

The officiating priest waves the two living sheep, on the eastern side of the altar before the presence of God. Though the language of the Mishnah seems to indicate that these sheep were waved by the priest simultaneously with the twin loaves, a simple interpretation of Maimonides seems to allow for the sheep being waved separately—perhaps on account of their great weight (c. 150 kg).

Waving the Twin Loaves and Sheep Parts Upon a Tray

Maimonides, in his monumental *Mishneh Torah*, writes, "The priest takes the breast and right hind leg of each of the two sheep and places them at the side of the twin loaves. He then places each of his two hands under them and waves them all together" (*T'midim U'Mussafim*, 8:11). Here, the priest makes use of a large tray for waving. Though neither Maimonides nor other authorities make any mention of such an instrument, its necessity appears to be self-evident.

Waving Parts of the Sheep with the Twin Loaves

According to the sages of the Mishnah, parts of the peace-offering were also waved *after* having been slaughtered. Rabbinic authorities reached differing conclusions as to the exact manner in which the twin loaves and the sheep had to be waved. This illustration reflects a literal understanding of the verse, "And the priest shall wave them upon the first harvest bread for a wave offering before the Lord . . ." (Lev. 23:20).

Priests Eating theTwin Loaves

Priests seated at tables in the Chamber of the Hearth, waiting to receive portions from the twin loaves and the peace-offerings. To the left, we can see the oven in which the two loaves were baked. In the doorway, two priests bring the loaves from the Temple Courtyard where they have just been waved. Each priest would actually receive only a very small portion of both the bread and the lamb. These offerings fell into the category of the "holiest of the holy" sacrifices (*Kodshei Kodashim*), and therefore certain regulations applied to them. For example, they had to be eaten on the day of their offering. In addition, they could only be eaten by male priests and only within the Temple Courtyard. In this illustration, the priests are seated in that side of the Chamber of the Hearth which was situated on the Temple Courtyard grounds.